Library of
Davidson College

REVOLUTION THROUGH REFORM

A Comparison of Sarvodaya and Conscientization

Mathew Zachariah

PRAEGER SPECIAL STUDIES • PRAEGER SCIENTIFIC

New York • Philadelphia • Eastbourne, UK
Toronto • Hong Kong • Tokyo • Sydney

Library of Congress Cataloging-in-Publication Data

Zachariah, Mathew.
  Revolution through reform.

  (The Praeger special studies series in comparative education)
  Bibliography: p.
  Includes index.
  1. Social movements. 2. Educational Sociology.
3. Social ethics. 4. Social change. I. Title.
II. Series.
HN18.Z28   1985   303.4′84   85-17023
ISBN 0-03-004528-2 (alk. paper)

Published in 1986 by Praeger Publishers
CBS Educational and Professional Publishing, a Division of CBS Inc.
521 Fifth Avenue, New York, NY 10175 USA

© 1986 by Mathew Zachariah

All rights reserved

6789   052   987654321

Printed in the United States of America on acid-free paper

INTERNATIONAL OFFICES

Orders from outside the United States should be sent to the appropriate address listed below. Orders from areas not listed below should be placed through CBS International Publishing, 383 Madison Ave., New York, NY 10175 USA

Australia, New Zealand
Holt Saunders, Pty. Ltd., 9 Waltham St., Artarmon, N.S.W. 2064, Sydney, Australia

Canada
Holt, Rinehart & Winston of Canada, 55 Horner Ave., Toronto, Ontario, Canada M8Z 4X6

Europe, the Middle East, & Africa
Holt Saunders, Ltd., 1 St. Anne's Road, Eastbourne, East Sussex, England BN21 3UN

Japan
Holt Saunders, Ltd., Ichibancho Central Building, 22-1 Ichibancho, 3rd Floor, Chiyodaku, Tokyo, Japan

Hong Kong, Southeast Asia
Holt Saunders Asia, Ltd., 10 Fl, Intercontinental Plaza, 94 Granville Road, Tsim Sha Tsui East, Kowloon, Hong Kong

Manuscript submissions should be sent to the Editorial Director, Praeger Publishers, 521 Fifth Avenue, New York, NY 10175 USA

*The Praeger Special Studies
Series in Comparative Education*

General Editor: ***Philip G. Altbach***

Published in Cooperation with the
Comparative Education Center,
State University of New York, Buffalo

ACADEMIC POWER: Patterns of Authority in Seven National Systems of Higher Education
John H. van de Graaff, Dietrich Goldschmidt, Burton R. Clarke, Donald F. Wheeler, Dorotea Furth

ADAPTATION AND EDUCATION IN JAPAN
Nobuo K. Shimahara

CHANGES IN THE JAPANESE UNIVERSITY: A Comparative Perspective
William K. Cummings, Ikuo Omano, Kazuyuki Kitamura

COMPARATIVE PERSPECTIVES ON THE ACADEMIC PROFESSION
Philip G. Altbach

FUNDING HIGHER EDUCATION: A Six-Nation Analysis
Lyman A. Glenny

US AND UK EDUCATIONAL POLICY: A Decade of Reform
Edgar Litt, Michael Parkinson

UNIVERSITY AND GOVERNMENT IN MEXICO: Autonomy in an Authoritarian System
Daniel C. Levy

PUBLISHING IN THE THIRD WORLD: Trend Report and Bibliography
Philip G. Altbach, Eva-Maria Rathgeber

UNIVERSITIES AND THE INTERNATIONAL DISTRIBUTION OF KNOWLEDGE
Irving J. Spitzberg, Jr.

STUDYING TEACHING AND LEARNING: Trends in Soviet and American Research
Robert Tabachnick, Thomas S. Popkewitz, Beatrice Beach Szekely

INTERNATIONAL BIBLIOGRAPHY OF COMPARATIVE EDUCATION
Philip G. Altbach, Gail P. Kelly, David H. Kelly

SYSTEMS OF HIGHER EDUCATION IN TWELVE COUNTRIES: A Comparative View
Nell P. Eurich

ADULT EDUCATION AND TRAINING IN INDUSTRIALIZED COUNTRIES
Richard E. Peterson, John S. Helmick, John R. Valley, Sally Shake Gaff, Robert A. Feldmesser, H. Dean Nielsen

WOMEN'S EDUCATION IN DEVELOPING COUNTRIES: Opportunities and Outcomes
Audrey Chapman Smock

THE SCIENCE PROFESSION IN THE THIRD WORLD: Studies from India and Kenya
Thomas Owen Eisemon

NONFORMAL EDUCATION AND NATIONAL DEVELOPMENT: A Critical Assessment of Policy, Research, and Practice
John Charles Bock, George John Papagiannis

EDUCATION IN THE ARAB WORLD
Byron G. Massialas, Samir Ahmed Jarrar

BETTER SCHOOLS: International Lessons for Reform
John Simmons

EDUCATION AND SOCIAL CHANGE IN THE PEOPLE'S REPUBLIC OF CHINA
John N. Hawkins

EDUCATION AND INTERGROUP RELATIONS: An International Perspective
John N. Hawkins and Thomas J. La Belle

RESEARCH ON FOREIGN STUDENTS AND INTERNATIONAL STUDY: An Overview and Bibliography
Philip G. Altbach, David H. Kelly, and Y. G-M. Lulat

For
Saro and Mamma

PREFACE

On a wintry 1981 January morning in Calgary I read an article by my friend David Radcliffe which mentioned that Sarvodaya and Conscientization were similar concepts. For the next four years, I attempted to find out the extent to which these two concepts and movements were similar. This volume presents the results of that search. A preliminary version of my conclusions was presented at a Calgary Humanities Institute lecture on March 24, 1982. A more recent version was presented on February 12, 1984, at the Annual Meeting of Western Anthropology Sociology Association in Regina, Saskatchewan, Canada.

When Paulo Friere visited Calgary in the summer of 1982 as a guest of the Faculty of Education, I explored with him in a video-taped interview several issues that had surfaced in my study. In 1984, Com/Media, The University of Calgary produced a 45-minute edited version from the original two-hour interview for commercial distribution.

I wrote the book because of my dissatisfaction with aspects of "modernization" and "dependency" theories that attempt to explain the need for, as well as the movements for, fundamental change in many parts of the world, especially Africa, Asia, and Latin America. It contends, at least implicitly, that many movements for fundamental social change must be viewed as attempts to revitalize indigenous cultures. Then, one would not, for example, make the Eurocentric error of seeing the billions of people in the "Third World" as having to choose between the variants of capitalism and communism. A recurring theme in the book is that ethical philosophies and social movements are the products of the experience of members of a society living in a particular time and place and that the attempts of people to transcend these culturally set limitations, mainly expressed in religious terms, deserve careful and respectful study.

I began this comparative study as a Fellow at the Calgary Institute for the Humanities, The University of Calgary in September 1981. A University of Calgary Killam Resident Fellowship which freed me from all teaching responsibilities from September through December 1984 enabled me to complete this work. Between 1981 and 1984, I reviewed quite systematically the considerable body of original and exegetical writings on Sarvodaya and Conscientization. Some of the original materials were in university libraries in Toronto, Chicago, and Berkeley which I was able to visit with a University of Calgary research grant. Miss J. Schmidt and Miss C. Calder at the Ontario Institute for Studies in Education were of much help when I perused "The Paulo Freire resource collection for studies in cultural action" at the OISE library. Kenneth R. Logan at the University of California, Berkeley libraries and William J. Alspaugh at the University of Chicago libraries helped me to find the necessary materials on Sarvodaya from their comprehensive South Asia holdings. Librarians at the University of Calgary were, of course, invariably helpful.

I take pleasure in acknowledging the support and assistance of many other individuals at the University of Calgary: Harold G. Coward, director, and Gerry Dyer, administrative assistant, of the Calgary Institute for the Humanities; Rodolph L. Schnell, head of the Department of Educational Policy and Administrative Studies and Robert F. Lawson, dean of the Faculty of Education. Jeanne M. Keech, friend and colleague-secretary typed and retyped several drafts of the chapters. I am happy to express my admiration for her patience, good humor and, above all, rare competence. Jagruti V. Dholakia prepared the name and subject indexes.

Many others, too numerous to mention by name, have offered encouragement and wise counsel during the course of researching and writing this book. I shall, however, be remiss not to mention two individuals: the Rev. Canon Charles Alexander of St. James Anglican Church, Calgary and John L. McNeill, friend and colleague. I should also acknowledge with thanks the critical comments and suggestions on Chapters 3, 4, and 7, respectively, of Graham Knox, Rebecca Larson, and Miriam Zachariah. Philip G. Altbach, general editor of this series and Lynda Sharp, my editor at Praeger, provided much needed support at a crucial time.

I have dedicated this book to Saro, my wife, and my mother, Mary Zachariah. It is also offered in gratitude to the memory of my father, M. G. Zacharias, as well as my mother's older sister, Aley S. Cherian and her husband, Samuel Cherian who "adopted" me and brought me up from the age of seven. Rabindranath Tagore, India's Nobel Laureate, once wrote that every new-born baby brings to the world the message that God has not yet despaired of the human race. I would like to address this book, therefore, to the newer generation, particularly my four children: Miriam, Benjamin, Philip, and Alexander.

Calgary, Alberta, Canada

CONTENTS

Preface		vii
List of Tables and Figure		xii
1	Themes and Theses	1
2	Sarvodaya in India: A Historical Introduction	12
3	Conscientization in Brazil: Origins and Development	28
4	The Religious Basis of Sarvodaya and Conscientization	40
5	The Challenges of Marxism and Nationalism	55
6	Education in Sarvodaya and Conscientization	68
7	Economics and Fundamental Technological Change	81
8	Proposals for Implementation: Critiques and Opposition	90

9	Comparing Revitalization Movements: Dimensions, Benefits, Pitfalls	102
10	The Dilemmas of Revolution Through Reform	116
Bibliography		130
Name Index		139
Subject Index		141
About the Author		148

LIST OF TABLES AND FIGURE

Tables

6-1 Steps in Conscientization	74
6-2 Before and After Conscientization	79
10-1 Summary Comparison of Sarvodaya and Conscientization	118

Figure

| 2-1 A Systematization of Satyagraha | 19 |

1

THEMES AND THESES

The title of this book contains an apparent contradiction. Crane Brinton, after noting that "revolution is one of those looser words" writes that it usually means "drastic, sudden substitution of one group in charge of the running of a territorial political entity for another group" (1960 pp. 3, 4). Such substitution often entails fundamental changes in the ideas and institutions of society. The phrases associated with reform, on the other hand, are: repair, improve, amend, remove faults, end abuses, and so on. The emphasis is not on the forceful replacement of those in power or the ruling ideas or even the prevalent patterned and fairly predictable way of doing things (that is, institutions) by new leaders, ideas, or practices but in correcting them gradually and through legitimate challenges. Reform means change for gradual betterment. Can reforms lead, without the high cost of violence and terror associated with revolutionary upheavals, to the kinds of changes that some reformers and many proponents of revolution agree are long overdue? This book, definitely, cannot offer a conclusive answer to that perennially debated question. It does, however, examine two ethical philosophies—Sarvodaya and Conscientization—which assert that a sincere, concerted attempt to transform human nature and social institutions must be made. In other words, Sarvodaya and Conscientization have revolutionary goals. But, as we shall see later, by eschewing violence (in the case of Sarvodaya) and by not directly promoting violence (in the case of Conscientization), they have earned the earmarks of reform movements. The strategy and tactics of reform movements are predicated on giving a nudge to the evolutionary progress of society. The most important theme in this book is the examination of the apparent contradiction of promoting revolution through reform, particularly through persuasion.

Many organizations proclaim in their constitutions or charters of incorporation that they hope for change of heart and mind in individuals as well as the reconstruction of society. Some notable examples are the Salvation Army, the Methodist Church, and Young Men's as well as Women's Christian Associations. Some of their proclamations are taken seriously by advocates, adherents, and observers. Others are tacitly acknowledged to be mere window dressing.

It is obvious that I have taken the claims of Sarvodaya and Conscientization seriously. A brief discussion of the reasons is appropriate here.

In some important ways, the world has become one economic and political system (Wallerstein 1979). Phrases such as "the first world" and "the third world" allude to that relatively recent (that is, post-sixteenth century) international phenomenon. Since this phenomenon was led by—and was the consequence of—the emergence of the West* as a world power, Western values, attitudes, and ways of life have appeared to reign supreme in today's world. Indeed, as Cassius said of Julius Caesar in Shakespeare's play, the West "doth bestride the narrow world like a Colossus" and many non-Western societies appear to "walk under his huge legs, and peep about to find [themselves] dishonourable graves."

Yet, many individuals and groups in non-Western societies have responded to the dominance of the West not with abject surrender but with a defiant stance proclaiming the validity and value of their indigenous cultures. With a certain flamboyance, Amilcar Cabral said: "Repressed, persecuted, humiliated, betrayed by certain social groups which have come to terms with the foreigner, [indigenous] culture takes refuge in villages, in forests and in the minds of the victims of domination, weathering all storms to recover all its power of expansion and enrichment through the struggle for liberation" (1973, p. 14). The very term indigenous cultures means that a group of individuals share a strong sense of common identity based on their relationship to their environment and to each other, expressed in a distinct language, a land-based economy and identifiably different rituals and ceremonies that provide pattern and meaning to people's lives. It is such responses—not slavish imitation of the West, even if that were possible—that will even-

---

*I am aware that phrases like "the West" are extremely abstract generalizations; my attempt here is to make a case in very broad strokes.

tually reshape much of the material conditions and spiritual and social values of the billions of people in most of Africa, Asia, and Latin America. Sarvodaya and Conscientization are two such responses. A caveat must be entered here: these developments are possible only if the world does not become a mere cinder—a mass dishonorable grave for humankind—in the aftermath of a nuclear war.

Why would traditional, indigenous cultures persist? One important reason is that, although not organisms, cultures are, in some ways, like organisms. (Organisms die. Cultures do not, although they can sometimes disappear either abruptly or gradually.) They respond to the challenge posed by changing environments and other cultures. Their responses tend to be based on their own values and institutionalized behaviors. This is exemplified in the observation documented in several studies that when an invention is exported to another culture it undergoes several changes in the course of becoming part of the host culture. Rudolph and Rudolph in *The Modernity of Tradition: Political Development in India* (1967) document the fact that the Western tradition of political democracy has been undergoing significant changes in the course of its practice in India. They demonstrate how these changes make sense if, among other things, we recognize the dominance of caste in the Indian social order and not judge them as aberrations from the ideal of democracy, presumably practiced in the West. Revitalization movements—as we shall presently see—acknowledge, even if implicitly, the validity of some of the challenges to the traditional culture but attempt to cope with it in terms of its own native genius. Dealing with the dilemmas posed by that attempt is another recurrent theme in this book.

Indigenous cultures will persist, albeit in significant modified forms in some cases, for a more prosaic reason. LeVine points out that "families of basically traditional orientations are multiplying and transmitting their own cultural orientations more rapidly" than the rate at which national elites can indoctrinate them to accept the presumed benefits of industrialization and formal education (1963, p. 284).* Revitalization movements that begin with the premise that the existing cultural base deserves respect, therefore, merit greater attention than they have received, particularly from scholars who saw "modernity" and "tradition" as polar opposites.

---

*The clause beginning with "national elites..." in this sentence is mine, not LeVine's.

CULTURAL REVITALIZATION

Anthony F. C. Wallace defines a revitalization movement as "a deliberate, organized, conscious effort by members of a society to construct a more satisfying culture." His paper outlined "the concepts, assumptions, and initial findings of a comparative study of religious revitalization movements" (1956, pp. 265, 279). I have used the Wallace approach to compare Sarvodaya in India and Conscientization in Brazil. They are not, in the strict sense of the term, only *religious* revitalization movements, although, at base, their inspiration is clearly religious. Since Sarvodaya and Conscientization are primarily movements for political and socio-cultural change, I have used the term "leader," which Wallace also uses, in place of his preferred term, "prophet." There is nothing in Wallace's approach that ought to prevent us from examining other than religious revitalization movements using his concepts.

This study, however, is not an empirical anthropological or sociological study in the sense that it is not based on my fieldwork and primary data collection. It is a study of the ethical philosophies of Sarvodaya and Conscientization. It is primarily a work of theoretical and conceptual exploration. It compares and contrasts two philosophies which are indigenous responses to the problems of underdevelopment and development in an Asian and a Latin American society, although, of course, they have been influenced by the philosophies and experiences of other cultures.

India and Brazil are countries of incredible complexity and diversity. India, the seventh largest country in the world, is about the size of Europe. Hundreds of identifiable ethnic communities call India their home. The number of languages officially recognized in the constitution is 15. The 32 states and union territories contain some 600,000 villages in which 80 percent of the people live. India is known for wealthy maharajahs, modern industrialists, and businessmen. It is even better known for the desperate poverty of its vast majority in the villages and 2,600 urban areas. During the heyday of the Sarvodaya movement, in the mid-1950s, the population of India was about 400 million. Only about 20 percent of the population was literate at that time.

Brazil, the fifth largest country in the world, is almost as large as the United States of America. It takes up almost half of the South American continent. The population is concentrated in the coastal area which is but one of its five main topographical zones. Caucasians, blacks, native people, and mestizos are the principal racial and ethnic groups. The 23 states and territories contain many more urban areas than in India. In the early 1960s, when Conscientization became a growing movement, the population of Brazil was about 70 million, almost half of whom lived in urban areas. About 60 percent of the population was literate at that time. Brazil, like India, was—and continues to be—characterized by extreme differences in the distribution of wealth.

Kurien cites *Poverty in India* by V. M. Dandekar and N. Rath to document the fact that after almost two decades of planned economic development in India, poor people became poorer in absolute and relative terms (1974, p. 14). While the upper and middle income groups gained from planned development, the per capita consumption of poorer people (40 percent of the population) declined by as much as 15 to 20 percent in 1960 to 1968. The distribution of the benefits of economic growth was very skewed during the 1950s and 1960s and continues to be so even today.

No single statistical table can adequately represent the gulf between wealth and poverty in Brazil. One might, however, point to it: the difference between the upper and lower income levels was 225:1 in 1982. (For a graphic description, see Coles 1981.) One of the shantytowns on the outskirts of Recife is called "Planet of the Apes." One inhabitant told a *Le Monde* journalist in late 1980 that whereas a Brazilian family needs 2,500 cruzerios a week, the typical average wage is 500 cruzerios. He continued: "When I get my weekly pay my sole impulse is to mug some passerby" (Niedergang 1980, p. 12). The statistics for the 1960s were just as bleak.

No one can do full justice to social movements in these two countries in a volume of this size. Let me, therefore, reiterate that the focus of this work is on theoretical comparison.

Revitalization movements necessarily imply the formulation and articulation of assertions about the relationships of human beings to each other and their material world. These assertions are, in a significant sense, hewn out of the experience of members of that society living in a particular place and period. In Asia and Latin America, several movements emerged in the nineteenth and particularly in the twentieth century which, among others, took into account the colonial experience, the abysmal poverty of the masses of people, and the uniquely cultural ways of responding to these experiences and conditions to create better societies. Sarvodaya and Conscientization are two such movements. I have referred to them as revitalization movements because Wallace's definition succinctly describes them, as we shall see in succeeding chapters.

But there are two other reasons for discussing Sarvodaya and Conscientization as revitalization movements. Wallace's definition of revitalization movements acknowledges *the active role* of members of a culture to construct a more satisfying culture. This is entirely compatible with the stances of Sarvodaya and Conscientization. There is not even a hint of condescension in the definition, namely, that of members of a superior culture attempting to "modernize" members of an inferior culture. There is much that is valuable in the "dependency theory" which points to the dominance of the Western capitalist nations on "the third world." The principal spokesmen for Sarvodaya and Conscientization have used elements of dependency theory in their writings. But one of its greatest drawbacks is that it implicitly portrays the billions of human beings in Asia, Africa, and Latin America as puppets manipulated by a few powerful multinational corporations and Western governments (Zachariah 1979, p. 342). Revitalization theory obviously avoids such a characterization. Second, the definition and its later elaboration recognize dissatisfaction on the part of members toward their own culture and the possibility that the dissatisfaction could have arisen as a result of contact with other cultures. Protest is a manifest demonstration of dissatisfaction. Both Sarvodaya and Conscientization began as protest movements.

Although Sarvodaya and Conscientization have revolutionary goals, they were not movements in situations of *extreme* dislocation such as a long and totally debilitating war. Therefore, they did not become fully revolutionary movements. Hence, they may be more profitably examined using Wallace's approach, since his characterization of revitalization movements as disturbances to societal homeostasis means that they are reform movements.

Finally, it seems to me that Wallace's definition—despite its preference for viewing society in homeostatic terms—implicitly acknowledges the dialectic relationship of thought to action. We may begin explicating this point by referring to his concepts of the mazeway (psychological reality) and structural reality. To do justice to these concepts, it is necessary to briefly highlight some relevant points in Wallace's article.

"Revitalization movements" is an inclusive term that encompasses nativistic, reform, cargo cult, religious revivalist, messianic, and millenarian movements. Sarvodaya and Conscientization movements contain the sometimes contradictory elements of nativism (emphasizing the elimination of certain alien persons, customs, values, etc.), religious revivalism (emphasizing the recovery of customs, values, etc. thought to have been originally present and now lost), and vitalism (incorporation in one's culture of selected aspects of another culture).*

According to Wallace, there are certain identifiable stages in a revitalization movement.

In a *"steady state,"* the culture's socialization processes and methods of dealing with change work well enough so that the stresses for the individuals and for groups are tolerable.

Externally induced factors such as war, political subordination, economic exploitation, epidemics, etc. create intolerable *individual stress* which manifest themselves in conflicts.

The prolonged experience of stress leads to a period of *cultural distortion* when individuals and groups will make changes in their personal lives by adding or substituting behavioral elements. Wallace characterizes these changes as "regressive" and identifies them as "alcoholism, extreme passivity and indolence, highly ambivalent dependency relationships, intragroup violence, disregard of kinship and sexual mores, irresponsibility in public officials, states of depression and self-reproach and probably a variety of psychosomatic and neurotic disorders" (1956, p. 269). The *widespread* prevalence of these behaviors makes the culture "mutually inconsistent and interfering."

Cultural distortion can lead to the end of a society. *Revitilization movements* make their appearance to check the process of distortion and decay.

Wallace identifies seven tasks that a revitalization movement must accomplish.

1. Change the mental image that individuals have of themselves.
2. Often a prophet or some other type of leader appears who proclaims and thereby communicates to others the need for this change based on his vision of a better society.
3. People who are persuaded by the leader develop a threefold organization—of leader, trusted disciples, and followers—to spread the message. At this point, the message becomes embodied in a movement.
4. The movement encounters resistance. To keep it alive and to spread its influence, the leader will adapt the tenets of the movement in response to serious challenges. This may in-

---

*We may note parenthetically that the Social Credit Movement of the 1930s in the province of Alberta, Canada was a revitalization movement (see Hiller 1977).

clude reinterpretation as well as elimination of selected versions of the original vision.
5. The movement is successful if the whole population accepts the basic message of the leaders and disciples. It is partially successful if some significant groups of people accept the entire message or if most of the population accepts parts of the message. In any of these instances, some significant cultural change would have taken place.
6. The new patterns of thought and action are accepted as normal, as part of the routines of the new society.
7. A *new steady state* is achieved and the disappearance of the culture is, at least, postponed.

Wallace uses the term "mazeway" to embody the mental image mentioned in number 1 above. "The mazeway is nature, society, culture, personality, and body image, as seen by one person" (p. 266). The mazeway "acts in ways which reduce stress" for the individual in a society. In the period of cultural distortion, the mazeway cannot succeed in its attempts to reduce stress. Part of the challenge of the leader(s) of a revitalization movement is to enable individuals to reformulate their mazeways:

> Whether the movement is religious or secular, the reformulation of the mazeway generally seems to depend on a restructuring of elements and subsystems which have already attained currency in the society and may even be in use, and which are known to the person who is to become the prophet or leader. The occasion of their combination in a form which constitutes an internally consistent structure, and of their acceptance by the prophet as a guide to action, is abrupt and dramatic, usually occurring as a moment of insight, a brief period of realization of relationships and opportunities. These moments are often called inspiration or revelation. The reformulation also seems normally to occur in its initial form in the mind of a single person rather than to grow directly out of group deliberations (p. 270).

The mazeway is the "psychological reality" which in a later paper (Wallace and Atkins 1960, pp.75-76) is contrasted with "structural reality." It is "a world of meanings, as applied to a given society or individual, which is real to the [social scientist], but it is not *necessarily* the world which constitutes the mazeway of any other individual or individuals" (italics in the original).

The assumption of homeostasis that undergirds Wallace's approach prevented him from exploring one significant problem regarding structural reality. Part of the mazeway of an individual enables him or her to perceive "structural reality" too. These perceptions influence the social scientist—whether an ethnographer or an economist—in his or her own mazeways and perceptions of the mazeways of the subjects investigated. These mutual influences have consequences in the behaviors of persons. In other words, we can better understand Sarvodaya and Conscientization if we see them in dialectical relationship to their interactions with their material world. This is a third theme which underlies this book.

AN OVERVIEW

Sarvodaya became a popular word in India in the 1950s and early 1960s. The term was first used by Mahatma Gandhi in his autobiography. According to Adi H. Doctor (1967, p. 3): "It is also the title that Gandhi gave to his Gujarati translation of Ruskin's *Unto This Last*. Gandhi confirms Wallace's assertion that mazeway reformulation begins in a moment of inspiration or revelation. Referring to the profound influence of John Ruskin's book, Gandhi wrote: *Unto This Last* made it as clear as daylight for me [that a life of labor, that is, the life of the tiller of the soil and the handicraftsman is the life worth living]. I arose with the dawn, ready to reduce these principles to practice" (1940, p. 224). Vinoba Bhave extended the meaning of Sarvodaya to make it an ethical philosophy with practical implications. The *Bhoodan* and *Gramdan* (gifts of land by people or institutions to landless persons and communities) as well as *Shramdan* (gift of free labor for community efforts) movements attracted considerable interest in India, Sri Lanka, and around the world and have been the objects of scholarly analysis.

Conscientizacao is the term Paulo Freire applied to the process of teaching and learning in which illiterate peasant adults in the region of Recife in northeastern Brazil participated. Freire, too, mentions that the wide implications of the term struck him suddenly as soon as he heard it. This Portuguese word and its English cousins "Conscientization" and "consciousness raising" have become quite popular as a result of the translation of Freire's works and the discussion of the attempts to apply his literacy method. Denis Goulet identifies the elements of Freire's literacy method as:

> participant observation of educators "tuning in" to the vocabular universe of the people; their arduous search for generative words at two levels; syllabic richness and a high charge of experiential involvement; a first codification of these words into visual images which

stimulate people "submerged" in the culture of silence to "emerge" as conscious makers of their own "culture"; the decodification by a "culture circle" under the self-effacing stimulus of a coordinator who is no "teacher" in the conventional sense, but who has become an educator-educatee in dialogue with educatee-educators too often treated by formal educators as passive recipients of knowledge; a creative new codification, this one explicitly critical and aimed at action, wherein those who were formerly illiterate now began to reject their role as mere "objects" in nature and social history and undertake to become "subjects" of their own destiny (Freire 1973b, p. viii).

It should be evident even from the above quote that Freire's pedagogy is a means to achieve a better world—a world in which the oppressed and the oppressors will be authentic subjects, not alienated objects.

Like Sarvodaya, Conscientizacao too has been subjected to analysis and practice in many parts of the world. I know of no publicly available systematic attempt to compare and contrast these two philosophies. The major questions that have guided me in this attempt to review the significant literature are listed below.

1. What are the economic and political conditions in India and Brazil which, at least in part, led to the formulation of these two philosophies? What are the principal tenets of these philosophies? (Chapters 2 and 3)
2. To what extent is Sarvodaya rooted in or have affinities to Hinduism? To what extent is Conscientizacao rooted in or have affinities to Christianity? (Chapter 4)
3. How have other philosophies—that is, Marxism and nationalism—influenced or affected the development of these two philosophies? (Chapter 5)
4. What are their views about the relationship of technology and social change? (Chapter 6)
5. How do these philosophies define education and the role of schools in promoting or not promoting education? (Chapter 7)
6. What are the specific proposals in these philosophies for bringing about desirable change in society? What are the problems which emerged in attempts to implement these philosophies? (Chapter 8)
7. What is the most appropriate way to compare Sarvodaya and Conscientization? (Chapter 9)
8. What are the major theoretical and practical criticisms of these two philosophies? How valid are they? Are these two

philosophies relevant only to economically poor societies? Do they have a message for affluent societies? (Chapter 10)

I have depended very heavily on the writings of Gandhi (and his disciple Bhave) and Freire to discuss the theoretical bases and concepts of Sarvodaya and Conscientization. Yet, this is not a comparison of Gandhi (whose stature is immeasurably greater) and Freire. They appear in these pages as founders and spokesmen for movements for progressive change. Therefore, I have chosen not to burden the bibliography with an extensive list of their publications.

Finally, Sarvodaya has a more fully articulated and multifaceted ideology than Conscientization. This fact is reflected in the somewhat asymmetrical treatment of the two movements in this book.

2

SARVODAYA IN INDIA: A HISTORICAL INTRODUCTION

> I do not want my house to be walled in on all sides and my windows to be stuffed. I want the cultures of all lands to be blown about my house as freely as possible. But I refuse to be blown off my feet by any.
> Mahatma Gandhi (Bose 1948, p. 298)

If Mahatma Gandhi had not died on that fateful January 30, 1948, he would have been the leading light of India's Sarvodaya movement in the 1950s. For, as Geoffrey Ostergaard and Melville Currell state:

> Without Gandhi, India would undoubtedly, sooner or later, have achieved political independence, but without Gandhi there would have been no Sarvodaya movement (1971, p. 27).

ANTECEDENTS OF SARVODAYA

Sarvodaya and Satyagraha

The attainment of independence, for Gandhi, was only a necessary condition for creating a society for the welfare of all through Satyagraha. The two terms *Sarvodaya* and *Satyagraha* will be discussed later but we may make a preliminary observation. Satyagraha has been discussed in far greater detail than Sarvodaya in the voluminous literature on Gandhi. One important reason might well be that the call for self-awareness, self-purification, and development of personal strength in Satyagraha strikes a responsive chord in individuals, especially when not caught up in a mass movement. While this generalization is applicable to members of all societies, it is particularly apt in the case of Indians whose religious ethos emphasizes an individual's *dharma,* albeit to be worked out in a family and caste context. Sarvodaya, on the other hand, challenges the individual to work with other individuals to help create a more just and humane society which is a far more risky and anxiety-ridden matter, not to mention the considerable inconvenience such work entails. Yet Raghavan N. Iyer points to the important dialectical relationship between Satyagraha and Sarvodaya:

> [Gandhi's] concept of *satya,* with *ahimsa* as the means, determined his doctrine of *satyagraha* or active resistance to authority, while the concept of *ahimsa* with *satya* as the common end, enabled him to formulate his doctrine of *sarvodaya* or nonviolent socialism (1973, p. 252).

There can be no doubt that Gandhi wanted to help reconstruct Indian society. The final sentence of his 1941 pamphlet *Constructive Programme: Its Meaning and Place* (India, Gov't. of 1979, p. 166), direct precursor of the Sarvodaya movement, states unequivocally that the attainment of independence from Britain "without the constructive programme will be like a paralysed hand attempting to lift a spoon."

In this pamphlet, Gandhi listed 18 items for social action. These included: the building of communal unity, the removal of untouchability, the promotion of village industries (especially the cottage handspinning industry), the adoption of a new craft-centered elementary education, the introduction of universal adult literacy, and the promotion of economic equality. While all of the 18 items listed in the *Constructive Programme* are wholly worthy of consideration for improving the quality of life in India, to a reader in the 1980s, some of them (such as giving adequate care to leprosy patients without any reference to other aspects of health care) appear to be part of a "grab bag." Yet, Gandhi's statement on economic equality is worth quoting at some length:

> This last is the master-key to non-violent independence. Working for economic equality means abolishing the eternal conflict between capital and labour. It means the levelling down of the few rich in whose hands is concentrated the bulk of the nation's wealth on the one hand, and the levelling up of the semi-starved naked millions on the other. A non-violent system of government is clearly an impossibility so long as the wide gulf between the rich and the hungry millions persists. The contrast between the palaces of New Delhi and the miserable hovels of the poor labouring class nearby cannot last one day in a free India in which the poor will enjoy the same power as the

richest in the land. A violent and bloody revolution is a certainty one day unless there is a voluntary abdication of riches and the power that riches give and sharing them for the common good.

I adhere to my doctrine of trusteeship in spite of the ridicule that has been poured upon it. It is true that it is difficult to reach. So is non-violence. But we made up our minds in 1920 to negotiate that steep ascent. We have found it worth the effort. It involves a daily growing appreciation of the working of non-violence....[Congressmen] should ask themselves how the existing inequalities can be abolished violently or non-violently. I think we know the violent way. It has not succeeded anywhere.

This non-violent experiment is still in the making. We have nothing much yet to show by way of demonstration. It is certain, however, that the method has begun to work though ever so slowly in the direction of equality. And since non-violence is a process of conversion, the conversion, if achieved, must be permanent (1979, p. 158).

Historical Background

India is the home of one of the oldest continuing civilizations on earth. In its 5,000 years of history, the land and people of India have undergone many transformations as the result of invasions, conquests, changes of ruling dynasties, propagation of new religions, introduction of economic and technical innovations, development of new forms of artistic endeavors, and so on.

Yet, India's civilization maintained its continuity in many essential and fundamental ways. Perhaps the most important reason was that social life in India was organized around its more than 600,000 villages. In religious matters, Hinduism permitted—indeed encouraged—the development of beliefs, rituals, and practices that met local needs to believe. The *jati* (in contrast to the more abstract *varna*) form of the caste system ensured the more or less widespread acceptance among the people of a divinely ordered social hierarchy. Escape from the lower and most exploited levels of the hierarchy was possible for individuals only on the basis of performing one's caste dharma meticulously in this life so that one can be born into a higher *jati* in one's next incarnation. The economy of the villages was based on agricultural imperatives and cottage industries to meet the needs of the people for clothing, shelter, household utensils, etc. Urban centers existed, of course, but they were the seats of remote governments who collected taxes from villages for purposes such as administration and warfare, which made little sense to the villagers.

The arrival of the Portuguese, the first Europeans, in India in the sixteenth century began a process of cultural change that would affect even village life. We need not pause to examine in detail the manner in which the Portuguese, the Dutch, and the French attempts to colonize India came to naught and Britain became the predominant colonial power in India.

No event in India's history, perhaps, affected it as profoundly as the colonization of India by Britain. The reorganization of landownership so that the government could collect taxes more efficiently, the introduction of Western education by British missionaries, the construction of an elaborate system of railways and roads, the creation of a judicial system, etc., played a role in changing the landscape and people of India. But all of them perhaps pale in the face of the processes of imperial exploitation that the British government and corporations had established. Industrialization began in India and the rural areas became hinterlands that supported the major metropolitan centers such as Calcutta, Bombay, and Madras within India and Liverpool, London, and Manchester in England. Millions of peasants were transformed into tenants caught in vicious cycles of poverty, debts to moneylenders and landlords. The insularity of the villages was destroyed; villagers became pawns in the hands of brokers and stockholders in distant places. Ennui set in on a widespread scale.

The history of India's attempt to attain independence may well be dated from 1857, the year that many British historians have called the sepoy (footsoldier) rebellion and many Indian historians in the 1950s termed "the first war of Indian independence." We cannot linger to examine the history of that movement which became a mass movement under Mohandas K. Gandhi's leadership.

But it is important to note that beginning in the 1930s, there were two distinctly different approaches within the Indian National Congress about how to bring about the regeneration of India's economy and culture. The Gandhian view emphasized the revitalization of village life as the most important and urgent task. Jawahrlal Nehru was the major spokesman for the other view which emphasized industrialization and Soviet-style economic planning. Nehru became India's first prime minister in 1947. Gandhi died in 1948. The government of India began preparations for the First Five-Year Plan in the early 1950s. It is against this background that Vinoba Bhave began spreading the message of Sarvodaya.

EAST AND WEST MEET IN SARVODAYA

Is the ideology of Sarvodaya based on Hindu and Buddhist ethical principles? We shall discuss the religious dimensions of this question and the influence of Christ's teaching on Gandhi in Chapter 3, but a brief comment is in order here.

Gandhi's promotion of the constructive program and, later, Sarvodaya, places him within the broader movement begun in the late eighteenth century among Indians exposed to Western learning to revitalize and, where necessary, transform Indian values, beliefs, and institutions. This revitalization movement (as defined in Chapter 1) was in part a nativistic movement in the sense of, first, asserting the glory that was India before colonization and, second, rejecting the intrusion of many non-Indian (particularly Western) persons, customs, and values into Indian society. Bondurant's quote of Gandhi is apt:

> Swadeshi is that spirit in us which restricts us to the use and service of our immediate surroundings to the exclusion of the more remote. Thus...I must restrict myself to my ancestral religion....If I find it defective I should serve it by purging it of its defects. In the domain of politics I should make use of the indigenous institutions and serve them by curing them of their proved defects (1965, pp.106-7).

But, Gandhi's efforts to create a "more satisfying culture" was, in part, also profoundly influenced by Western precepts and examples. His understanding of the defects of his ancestral religion or traditional politics was often based on the acceptance of Western criteria and conclusions. An instructive example of the way Gandhi brought together east and west can be found in the term Sarvodaya.

According to Adi H. Doctor, Gandhi borrowed the term from an ancient Jaina Scripture by Acharya Samantabhadra (1967, p. 3). Gandhi points out in *His Own Story* that Sarvodaya is the title he gave to his Gujerati translation of John Ruskin's *Unto This Last*. Ruskin's book had profoundly influenced Gandhi. He learned, he claimed, three things from it:

1. The good of the individual is contained in the good of all.*
2. A lawyer's work has the same value as the barber's, inasmuch as all have the same right of earning their livelihood from their labour.
3. That a life of labour, i.e., the life of the tiller of the soil and handicraftsman is the life worth living.
    The first of these I knew. The second I had dimly realized. The third had never occurred to me. Ruskin made it as clear as possible

---

*Doctor reinterprets this as "That economy is good which conduces to the good of all."

for me that the second and third were contained in the first (1930, pp. 184–85).

Elizabeth T. McLaughlin in *Ruskin and Gandhi* (1974) mentions that Gandhi's familiarity with Ruskin's writings at least included *Fors Clavigera* where the concept of "bread labor" is enunciated. (See also Iyer 1973, p. 14.) Her conclusion is that "A number of scholars who have represented Gandhian economics as unique and original have overlooked its dependence upon the thought of Ruskin" (1974, p. 119). It is difficult to fully agree without knowing in specific terms the connotations of McLaughlin's use of the words "unique" and "original." Nevertheless, her argument that "Ruskin anticipated almost all the characteristic features of Gandhian economics" is quite persuasive.

Gandhi's writings contain references to many Westerners (for example, Sir Henry Maine and Thomas Carlyle) but here we shall discuss only the influence of Leo Tolstoy and Henry David Thoreau. Gandhi's indictment of modern, urban industrial society, his belief in the efficacy of non-violence, his promotion of "bread labor," and his preference for the negation of the state owe much to the sustenance he drew from Tolstoy's writings. Tolstoy's *The Kingdom of God is Within You* expressed a very important principle of life for Gandhi.

Gandhi had often referred to Thoreau's essay on civil disobedience in his discussions on the technique of Satyagraha. Bhattacharya states that "the Thoreauvian imprint on Gandhi was quite marked" (1969, p. 51). However, he also cites the influence of ancient Hindu philosophy on Ralph Waldo Emerson and Thoreau and asserts that Gandhi received back from America what was fundamentally the philosophy of India after it had been distilled and crystalized in the mind of Thoreau (p. 52). Gandhi refers to Thoreau's view "that that government is best which governs the least" as a classic statement (Kher 1957, vol. 1, p. 36).

Bondurant (1965, p. 106) is only partly correct in her assertion that Gandhi's views and perspectives had been deeply rooted in traditional India. Many of his specific views cannot be legitimately traced to traditional India. The 23 years Gandhi spent in England and South Africa led him, for instance, to the very un-Hindu view that all persons are equal in the eyes of God. The concept of anarchy in Gandhian politics provides us with another example of reinterpretation from a Western perspective. Doctor in *Anarchist Thought in India* asserts that ancient Indian political writings cannot be legitimately used to support Gandhian anarchism (1964, pp. 15-35). Ved Mehta's comment that Gandhi "saw Indian filth with the eyes of a foreigner" is also appropriate here (1976, p. 243).

A FEW KEY TERMS

The major concepts relevant to the discussion of the Indian cultural revitalization movement are Sarvodaya and Satyagraha. Gandhi and, later, Bhave, drew upon the *Gita* and the *Upanishads* to relate these concepts to a perfectible society.

The two constituent terms in Sarvodaya are *sarva* (all) and *udaya* (rising). The literal translation of Sarvodaya would then be "the rising of all." This rising has physical and material dimensions but at base it is spiritual enlightenment that brings about changes in the physical and material aspects. Gandhi's disciple Vinoba Bhave often said that both the rich and the poor are in a fallen state although for different reasons (Sharma 1960, p. 258). Says Bhave:

> A philosophy of life based on a penetrating insight into "the life of things" is essential for a revolution. The courage to penetrate and the power to see clearly the meaning of things hidden beyond the situation prevailing around us and to act up to the discovered meaning of what is known is revolutionary insight. That philosophy which is based on the insight into the special characteristics concealed within the womb of a given situation in history is revolutionary philosophy.... Revolution can take place only where there is this power of penetrating insight (1964, p. 1).

Although Gandhi translated *Sarvodaya* as "the welfare of all," such welfare would be the result of enlightenment.

Satyagraha has often been translated as "holding fast to the truth." No pithy phrase or sentence can do justice to this concept. Gandhi began practicing some form of Satyagraha in South Africa in the late nineteenth century before he and, later, others began to propound its conceptual and theoretical foundations. Although our brief exposition in the paragraphs to follow has a static quality, it is important to remember that there has been a *process* of praxis (reflection-action-reflection...) in the enrichment and refinement of Satyagraha as a means and as an end.

Naess (1974, p. 55) systematized the Satyagraha approach in this manner (see Figure 2-1):

FIGURE 2-1

A SYSTEMATIZATION OF SATYAGRAHA*

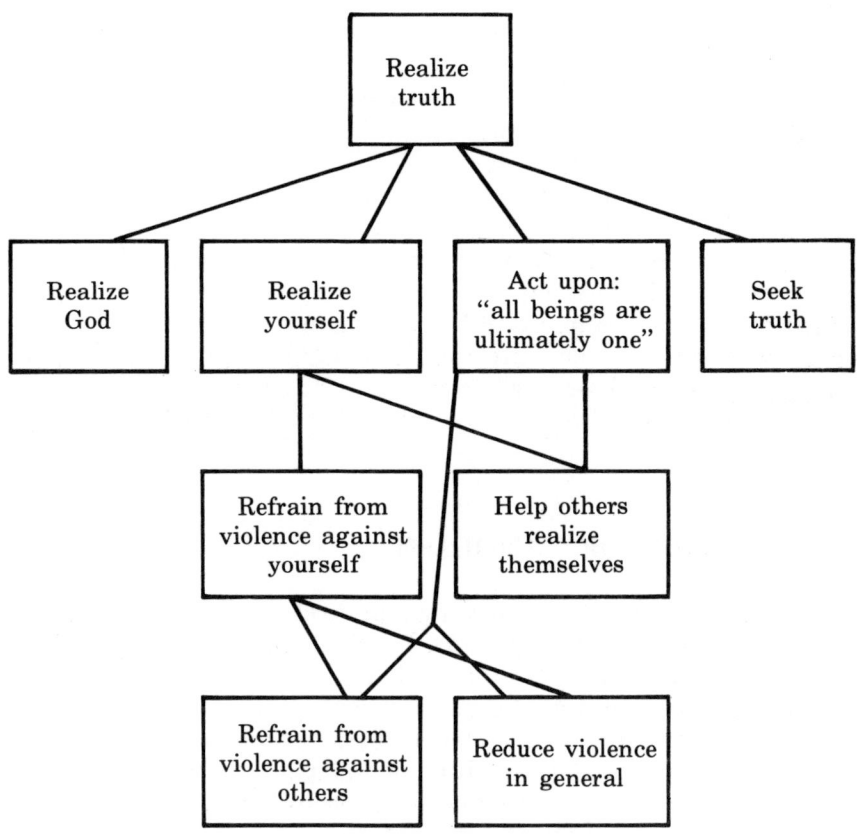

---

*This chart, while helpful, indicates that the concept is riddled with ambiguities.
Source: Arne Naess, *Gandhi and Group Conflict,* p. 55.

"Bread labor" is another important term in Sarvodaya. The principle tenet is that every individual must directly undertake manual labor to provide for oneself at least some of the basic necessities of life. This implies that everyone would be directly involved in working on the land in some way. Then, there will be enough of the basic necessities for everyone and everyone will have enough leisure to devote to mental and spiritual development. In a society in which everyone is required to labor for one's own bread, invidious caste and class distinctions would not arise. People will keep busy (which will improve their mental and physical health), they will have opportunities to commune with nature directly, and they will curb their wants. No one would be permitted to earn their bread, as it were, entirely by intellectual labor. Ideally, the main motivation for doctors, lawyers, and other "intellectual workers" would be service to humankind. The human triumph, said Gandhi once, "will consist in substituting the struggle for existence by the struggle for mutual service" (Narayan 1969, p. 333).

Several other terms and concepts will be discussed in Chapter 4.

THREE TYPES OF GANDHISM

Ostergaard and Currell distinguish three types of Gandhism in post-colonial India (1971, pp. 6-7). Political Gandhism attempts to achieve at least some of Gandhi's ideas through actions embodied in agitations, electoral politics, and government efforts to promote, for instance, *Panchayati Raj* (local self-government). Institutional Gandhism refers to the activities of independent and voluntary organizations that promote Gandhi's ideas and certain of his social action projects. An example is the Gandhi Peace Foundation in India which promotes research into the principles of non-violence. The third type is Revolutionary Gandhism. Its organizational base was the Akhil Bharat Sarva Seva Sangh (The All-India Association to Serve All the People) founded in 1949.

The Sarvodaya movement which Vinoba Bhave had guided for many years since Gandhi's death was an expression of revolutionary Gandhism with three major aims: to change the hearts and minds of people so that they may pursue truth; to enable people to practice a lifestyle which will encourage them to pursue truth; and, to change current social structures enough so that new, decentralized structures that facilitate personal pursuits of truth within a nurturing community are possible. It takes as a point of departure a statement Gandhi wrote a day before his death: "India has still to attain social, moral and economic independence in terms of its seven hundred thousand villages as distinguished from its cities and towns" (Bhattacharya 1969, p. 511). In this brief note (sometimes called "Last Will and Testament"), Gandhi recommends that the Indian National Congress organization should be disbanded and that it should "flower into a Lok Seva Sangh [People's Servants Society]." The following excerpts from it are especially significant.

> It should be noted that this body of servants derive their authority or power from service ungrudgingly and wisely done to their master, the whole of India.
> 1. Every worker shall be a habitual wearer of *khadi* made from self spun yarn...and must be a teetotaler. If a Hindu, he must have abjured untouchability in any shape or form in his own person or in his own family. [He] must be a believer in the ideal of inter-communal unity, equal respect and regard for all religions and equality of opportunity and status for all irrespective of race, creed or sex.
> 2. He shall come in personal contact with every villager within his jurisdiction.
> 3. He shall enrol and train workers from among the villagers and keep a register of all these.
> 4. He shall keep a record of his work from day to day.
> 5. He shall organize the villagers so as to make them self-supporting and self-contained through their agriculture and handicrafts.
> 6. He shall educate the village folk in sanitation and hygiene and take all measures for prevention of ill health and disease among them.
> 7. He shall organize the education of the village folk from birth to death along the lines of *Nayee Talim,* in accordance with the policy laid down by the Hindustani Talimi Sangh (Bhattacharya 1969, pp. 511-12).

Gandhi categorically states that if the rich do not become trustees of their wealth and share it with the poor,

> nonviolent noncooperation and civil disobedience [is] the right and infallible remedy, *for the rich cannot accumulate wealth without the cooperation of the poor in society* (Kher 1957, vol. 1, p. *xlv;* emphasis added).

Two features of revolutionary Gandhism, the principle of anarchism and the focus on rural areas, require elucidation.

Although there were very many poor and destitute people in India's urban centers, the overwhelming majority of them lived in villages. Gandhi saw serving them as serving *daridranarayana,* that is, God as manifested in the poor and the lowly. Furthermore, Gandhi was convinced that the real genius of India resided—relatively unscathed from colonization and the ravages of war—in the villages:

> If the village perishes India will perish too....We have to make a choice between India of the villages that are as ancient as herself and India of the cities which are a creation of foreign domination (Gandhi 1952, p. 3).

Third, Gandhi was convinced that centuries of foreign domination had sapped India's villages of all their vitality and destroyed their "republican" character. The severe problems of the villages, such as poverty, unemployment, underemployment, illiteracy, exploitation of the poor by the rich, poor sanitation, poor productivity, etc. had to be urgently tackled. He was convinced that a revolutionary change was necessary to rejuvenate India's villages. He wished to have it brought about through *Sarvodaya,* for, otherwise the poor exploited peasants would resort to violent and destructive means which may not bring about any improvement. Gandhi's critique of foreign domination is in many respects similar to the "metropolis-hinterland" approach which in the 1960s became popular in Latin America. He was familiar with R. C. Dutt's two-volume study *The Economic History of India* published in 1902 and 1904 which documented in rich detail Britain's exploitation of India. For instance, his main criticism of the railways built by the British was that they had destroyed the relative self-sufficiency of the villages and had converted them into hinterlands for the metropolises in India and Britain (Kher 1957, p. *vii*). Moreover, Gandhi was convinced that only if one lived close to the land as most people do in villages could one practice the principle of "bread labor." Finally, in the village it is possible for human beings to be in touch with each other and avoid the problems of massification and alienation that plague urban centers.

Gandhi's views on the necessity to revive the tradition of village republics have generated much discussion of his anarchist views (Ostergaard and Currell 1971, pp. 32-45; Doctor 1964). The individual was to be at the center of political organization for Gandhi which meant that the organization ought to be small enough for the individual to influence it. Gandhi also insisted that linking of villages with each other must not result in a hierarchy but must be perceived as an oceanic circle. The state by definition was for Gandhi—as for Western anarchists—an instrument of manipulation and coercion. Gandhi's and his disciple Vinoba Bhave's anarchism anticipated the later "small is beautiful" school of thought in the West.

Vinoba Bhave

Preoccupation with the struggle for Indian independence prevented Gandhi from promoting Sarvodaya in the 1930s and 1940s. It, therefore, fell to Vinoba Bhave to take up the cause when Gandhi fell to an assassin's bullet. Acharya Vinoba Bhave was widely acknowledged as Gandhi's "spiritual heir" at the time of the latter's death.

Although Gandhi never tried to hide the fact that his concept of Sarvodaya was revolutionary, it fell to his disciple Bhave to make its revolutionary character explicit in a number of ways. For instance, Gandhi often told the rich that they held their wealth in trusteeship for all members of society. The only practical implication was that the rich who hold private property must engage in charitable works. Vinoba Bhave interpreted the concept of trusteeship in terms of the village or local community. The implication was that property must be *held* in common. Second, Gandhi was a vehement opponent of the abuses of the caste system, particularly the concept of ritual pollution and the inhumane treatment of untouchables. But he did not oppose the *varna* system if it could be rid of its brutality. Bhave, on the other hand, argued vehemently for the abolition of caste and had in fact confined his sacred threat (which identified him as a Brahmin) to the fire very early in his life. Third, in Vinoba's writings the concept of enlightened anarchy has been emphasized a great deal more than in Gandhi's works. These differences, however, should not lead us to ignore the continuity and basic harmony of Gandhi's and Vinoba's thoughts.

Vinoba Bhave was born in 1895 in Gagoda, now in Maharashtra, and died in 1982. The Bhaves were Brahmins of upper middle class standing. Lanza del Vasto mentions that during his youth Vinoba used to spend long hours in country walks. Says Lanza del Vasto:

> [Vinoba] was troubled whenever he passed through a village. Not that there was the slightest sign of unrest amongst the villagers he peered at through his spectacles. It was their calm rather which troubled him, the calm of stagnation (1974, p. 15).

Lanza del Vasto also quotes a soliloquy Vinoba wrote in 1915:

> Sloth, fear and ignorance explain everything we are. What has done this to us? A century of slavery has done it.... But where is our master to be found so that we may leap at his throat? The Englishman is here, but only as though he were not. Every time the Indian would get at him, he finds only another Indian who smites him...like the man who, turning around, slaps his own face because of a mosquito which has flown away (1974, pp. 15-16).

Since Vinoba had excelled in mathematics, his father, an admirer of Western learning, had wanted him to study engineering in England. But Vinoba did not accept the suggestion. In 1916, on his way to appear for the Intermediate Examination* in Bombay, he detrained at Surat and went to Calcutta and Banares where he studied Sanskrit and became proficient in Hindu scriptures with the help of pandits (men of learning). He spoke ten Indian languages as well as Arabic and Persian. He also spoke and wrote in English and French.

It is said that in his late teens Vinoba had associated with a group of young men who planned a series of violent acts against the British. He had, till 1915, carried with him the aspiration to kill at least one Englishman to avenge the British colonization of India. But in 1916, he met Gandhi who, he says, "cured me of that desire. It is he who extinguished the volcano of anger and passion which was ever alive in me." In the midst of a later paean of praise of the English, Bhave said, "I have known some good Christians among them and, there is no worthier object of love than a good Christian [Englishman]" (Lanza del Vasto 1974, p. 22).

Although Vinoba had been jailed for participating in civil disobedience movements in the 1920s and 1940s, he did not become a well-known public figure until 1951 when he began to promote *Bhoodan* (gifts of land).

THE ORIGINS OF BHOODAN

It is necessary to mention in some detail the manner in which the Sarvodaya concept became a potentially revolutionary social movement. The third annual meeting of the Sarva Seva Sangh was

---

*This examination was usually taken after two years of college attendance following high-school graduation. If a student passed, he may proceed with further study for the first degree.

held in Hyderabad City in 1951. The decision to hold the meeting in Hyderabad was itself a response to the violence between the peasants and landlords in Telengana, in the eastern half of the erstwhile princely state of Hyderabad. The peasants of Telengana had been forming a revolutionary movement there under Communist party leadership since 1947. The semi-feudal agrarian system under which the peasants were exploited had provided fertile soil for such radical leadership. The communists were, for a brief period, in alliance with the Congress party when both groups considered the Nizam (king) of Hyderabad their common enemy. After the Nizam was overthrown through a military action and an interim Congress government was established, the communists refused to surrender their arms. They forcibly took land from landlords and divided it among landless peasants. They claimed that they had "Sovietized" 3,000 villages and that 1 million acres of land were seized by the peasants (Oommen 1972, p. 28). A large number of people died during this period at the hands of either the armed communists or the police. Eventually, the police won the bitter 1949–50 struggle. Vinoba decided to walk back to his ashram via Telengana after the meeting in Hyderabad in 1951. He stopped at Pochampalli to give a talk on peace. After his talk, a group of so-called untouchables apparently said to him:

> We, too, love peace, but we are workers and have no land to work. What do you want us to do? Instead of talking to us about peace, give us land and we'll always live in peace (Lanza del Vasto 1974, p. 85).

Bhave asked the rich men in the gathering if they would be willing to listen to the poor people's plea and donate some land to them. It is important to note that in the Hindu spiritual tradition gift-giving is not to be equated with patronizing charity.* Touched

---

*An incident from Vinoba's reminiscences about his childhood illustrates the Hindu orientation very well:

"There's a big fat fellow come begging," I told my mother once. "Giving alms to people like that encourages idleness," and I quoted the Gita in support of my saying. My mother replied: "The beggar at the door is God in person. Suppose, now, you try to distinguish between deserving and undeserving cases. Are you going to treat God as an undeserving case?..."

"Up to now I have found no answer to this reasoning," is Vinoba's comment (Lanza del Vasto 1974, p. 20).

by Vinoba's call, a landowner, Ramachandran Reddy, stood up and donated 100 acres of his land. Thus was born the *Bhoodan* movement. For many years after that signal day, Bhave undertook *padayatra,* that is, he walked from village to village attempting to persuade landowners to donate a portion of their land for distribution to landless laborers who were and continue to be the poorest people in rural India. In the early years, the targets were exceeded; therefore, a target of 50 million acres for 1957 was set. However, by the end of that year only 4.2 million acres were donated. Sad to say, of these, 1.85 million was found to be uncultivable or legally disputed land. Obviously, many individuals who gave "gifts" to the movement did not do so out of noble motives. Neither, I venture to say, did the many members of the elite who encouraged the movement.

Meanwhile, the *Bhoodan* movement was widened to become *Gramdan* (the gift of the village) which represented a significant shift in perspective. Ostergaard and Currell state:

> In its Bhoodan campaign the movement asked landowners to donate one-sixth of their land for redistribution to landless labourers. The concept of Gramdan grew naturally out of Bhoodan as a consequence, so to speak, of "over-subscription" by the landowners of a village. The first village to "oversubscribe" to such an extent as to change Bhoodan into Gramdan was Mangroth in Utter Pradesh....The largest landowner, the head man of the village, was Diwan Shatrughana Singh. His decision to donate all his land to Bhoodan inspired the other landowners in the village, excepting one smallholder...to do likewise. The land so given was vested in the village community, and subsequently redistributed among the villagers in amounts which varied with each family's capacity and need (1971, p. 52).

The complete surrender of individual property rights in favor of the village community is, without doubt, a radical step. For that reason, *Gramdan* met with considerable resistance and made very little progress. Meanwhile, Bhave exhorted people to donate their labor *(Shramdan)*, their intelligence *(Budhidan)*, etc. to raise the quality of life of the poorest of the poor.

SARVODAYA TODAY

The Sarvodaya movement lost much of its appeal and force by the early 1960s. The word *Sarvodaya* and a movement to promote it have become popular again after their almost total eclipse in the 1960s. This revival is not taking place in India, but in neighboring Sri Lanka where almost the entire emphasis is on *Shramdan,* the voluntary provision of labor by mostly middle-class youth to assist poor people in villages. Like Buddhism which originated in India but was suffocated there only to thrive in Ceylon, southeast and east Asia, the Sarvodaya movement has, in effect, expired in India. The Sarva Seva Sangh, the organization founded to promote Sarvodaya, for all practical purposes, merely exists. The government of India's proud claim that India is now the ninth or tenth most industrialized country in the world is positive proof of the demise of the vision and program of the men who would have revived India's villages where men, women, and children could grow or make for themselves the basic necessities of life, directly participate in the governance of their community, and encourage each other to develop their intellectual and spiritual potential.

3

CONSCIENTIZATION IN BRAZIL: ORIGINS AND DEVELOPMENT

When I give food to the poor, they call me a saint. When I ask why the poor have no food at all, they call me a communist.

Dom Helder Camara

If the origins of Sarvodaya can be traced to Mahatma Gandhi, the broad Brazilian movement for *Conscientizacao* (translated as Conscientization, hereinafter) cannot similarly be traced to one person. Several individuals including the philosopher and theologian Henrique de Lima Vaz, SJ had provided the theoretical basis for the Movement for Basic Education (Movimento de Educacao de Base) in the 1950s and early 1960s (de Kadt 1970, p. 70). In Brazil, as in India, there were peasant rebellions in the late nineteenth and early twentieth centuries. The Catholic Church was aware of the widespread dissatisfaction of peasants and workers, particularly in northeast Brazil in the 1950s. Many church leaders expressed the need to respond constructively to this dissatisfaction. One of them, Dom Helder Camara had provided extremely valuable support for "liberation theology" which was one of the moving forces behind the urge to reconstruct Brazilian society. But just as in the case of Sarvodaya as a social movement, we have paid particular attention to one of its proponents, Vinoba Bhave, in the later part of this chapter, we shall focus on one of Conscientization's principal theoreticians and practitioners, Paulo Freire.

HISTORICAL BACKGROUND

A Portuguese explorer, Pedro Alvares Cabral, discovered Brazil for the Europeans in 1500 as a result of a navigational error. Unlike the history of India which can be counted in millenia, Brazilian history, for our purposes, begins with European colonization. Freire asserts that Latin America's—including, of course, Brazil's—

> colonisation consisted of transplantation by the invaders. Its population was crushed; its economy was based upon slave labor (particularly that of Negroes brought from Africa as [chattels]); it was dependent upon foreign markets, and usually followed a cyclic pattern. Moreover, its economic structures, biased from the beginning in favor of the conquerors, were based on natural resources which were systematically exploited and directed toward European markets. The economic, social, political and cultural control of the colonizing centers—Spain and Portugal—molded the Latin American societies into both agrarian and exporting societies, subject to a rural oligarchy, initially transplanted and always dependent upon foreign interests.
> During the colonial period, we were "closed societies", slaveowning, without a constituency, mere "reflection".*
> The prevailing kind of economic domination determined a culture of domination which, once internalized, meant submissive behavior by the dominated (1970, p. 169).

The economic and cultural domination was in part a legacy of the "patron-dependent" or "patron-client" relationship which pervades "certain significant and widespread patterns of behaviour in Brazil" (de Kadt 1970, p. 9). Says Dewitt:

> The *engenho de acucar* [the sugar plantation] was not only the foundation of a new economy, it was also the organizing principle of the family, the society and the culture as well (1971, p. 20).

This feudal system, symbolized also by the *Casa Grande* (Great Mansion) became the force for unifying the diverse cultures of the Portuguese, Amerindians, and Africans not only in northeastern Brazil but throughout the country. Gilberto Freyre describes this as a "system of relations of men and nature with each other, characterized by the predominance of the patriarchal organization in the family, the society and the economy, whose system of labor revolved around the productiveness of the slave" (Dewitt 1971, p. 21). Dewitt points out that the five symbols, namely, the *parentela* (patriarchal organization of the family), the *engenho de acucar,* the *mansions* of plantation owners, the *shanties,* and the *chapel* and their mutual relationships represent accurately the social formation of most of

---

*The traditional, caste-based village republics which Gandhi extolled in his writings were "closed societies" too. But in Sarvodaya, the rejuvenated village republics would be open to healthy influences from the outside, said Gandhi.

Brazil. Several authors trace this relationship to the manner and style of operation of the owners, *senhores de engenho,* of plantations in northeastern Brazil which, for purposes of manageability, is the only area I shall discuss to illustrate the problems of Brazil:

> Inevitably, the political system that evolved from this neofeudal structure was designed to uphold it. Certain *senhores de engenho* in the sugar zone and large landowners throughout the rest of the Northeast assumed the role of political bosses in their immediate environs. They became known as *coroneis* (colonals) (Page 1972, p. 20).

Recife, the largest, most important city in northeastern Brazil, is also capital of the state of Pernambuco. It is known as the Brazilian Calcutta, a phrase which immediately evokes pictures of unnecessary and untimely death as well as urban decay and the degeneration of the social fabric. Recife is the urban expression of a larger and widespread deprivation in the sugar zone, the coastal cities, the backlands, and a transitional zone known as the *agreste* (Page 1972, p. 15).

The northeastern region, which has been the least developed area in all of Brazil—except from about 1500 to 1654 when sugar production ensured an era of affluence—experienced the problems of economic and cultural dependency even more acutely than other regions.* From the earliest times of colonization, the Portuguese had followed a pattern of exclusively growing sugar cane there to take full advantage of the rich, black, *massape* (coastal region) soil (Barnard 1980, p. 14). Although there were times when sugar production enormously enriched the coffers of the landowners, it did not benefit the peasants who labored in *latifundia* ruled by an aristocracy. Barnard claims that:

> The exclusive devotion to sugar led the landowners to destroy the natural forest and wildlife of the coastal areas almost completely, so that the diet of the plantation workers was impoverished, often consisting largely of manioc, a tuber which grows easily but is low on nutritional value. Since sugar growing demanded increasing amounts of land, food cultivation was forced onto more and more marginal soil, closer to the [dry hinterland]. And in a conflict over whether to grow sugar for export or food for the workers, the outcome was rarely in doubt. Figures on land tenure throw some light on this: in 1956,

---

*In 1955, the state of Sao Paulo, with its population of 10,330,000 inhabitants, had a gross product 2.3 times larger than the entire northeast, whose population for the same year was 20,100,000. The per capita income in the Sao Paulo region was consequently 4.7 times higher than that of the northeast (Furtado 1963, p. 265).

twenty percent of the rural inhabitants owned land; the other eighty percent were renters, sharecroppers and the like. Half of the land in the northeast was owned by three percent of the population. Partly as a result, per capita income in the northeast was only forty percent of the national average (1980, p. 19).

It is necessary to omit here more detailed discussion of many facets of Brazil's development such as the abolition of slavery in 1888, the establishment of the Republic in 1889, and the politics of President Getulio Vargas from 1930 to 1945 as well as his second presidency from 1951 to 1954, the last being the year in which he committed suicide.

In 1953, as part of his masterful balancing act, Vargas had brought into his cabinet Joao Goulart, a young leftist with close links to trade unions. Goulart became president in 1960. The late 1950s and early 1960s were periods of turmoil in all of, but particularly northeastern, Brazil. Freire has referred to this period, perhaps too optimistically, as the beginning of the end of the "closed society" and the beginning of a "society in transition." Goulart had encouraged the organization of unions and had proposed agricultural and other kinds of reform. The late 1950s and the early 1960s were a period of new political activity in Brazil which raised the hope that a new Brazil could come into existence. The major issues were to end the "giveaway" of Brazilian resources, particularly to restrict the repatriation of profits by transnational corporations, and to ensure the participation of all adult Brazilians, including illiterates, in elections and land reform.

The Movimento de Cultura Popular and Freire's literacy campaign are examples of reform-minded political activity. They had their antecedents in a peasant movement which was underway in northeastern Brazil between 1955 and 1964. This Peasants' Leagues (*ligas camponesas*) movement was started by a plantation tenant, Jose de Prazeres, and had gained considerable support among the peasantry.* By 1961 it became clear that this movement was aimed at significant changes. The Peasants' Leagues movement had the support of Francisco Juliao, a state legislator who, despite his upper class origins, was sympathetic to the peasants' plight. As in other parts of Brazil, there was an air of optimism in northeastern Brazil in the late 1950s and early 1960s: optimism generated by a government agency—Superintendency for the Development of the

---

*Joseph A. Page's description of events in northeastern Brazil, written from an enlightened American perspective, is a pleasure to read (Page, *The Revolution That Never Was*).

Northeast (SUDENE)—directed by an internationally respected Brazilian economist, Celso Furtado. Miguel Arreas, who had spearheaded the Movimento de Cultura Popular in Pernambuco and was mayor of Recife had become governor of the state in 1963. He put an end to the lawless behavior of the landlords which had often resulted in indiscriminate killing of peasants by death squads and torture of others who protested unjustified eviction and other misdeeds. He successfully insisted that the police be impartial in meting out punishment and that they should not "automatically" favor the landlords. He also supported the strikes by peasants and sugarcane workers for decent minimum wages and regular working hours. The strikes succeeded in their goals, partly because Brazil could demand a higher price from the United States for sugar. The reason: the United States did not want to trade with its traditional supplier, Cuba, which had had a successful socialist revolution in 1959.

The Catholic Church began organizing peasant unions, among other things, to counter the influence of the Peasants' Leagues (Bruneau 1974). The church-sponsored unions emphasized education programs that would assist peasants to overcome their cultural backwardness (Mies 1973, p. 1,765). It supported President Goulart's efforts in the early 1960s to bring about reforms and contain the extreme radical elements in the northeast. In fact, the church, especially since the early 1950s, had repeatedly called for basic social reforms. Freire has been accused of being a Marxist. Yet de Kadt in *Catholic Radicals in Brazil* says that it was at least partly in reaction to the increasing influence of communists in the Popular Culture Movement that Freire transferred his work to promote political democracy to the Cultural Extension Service of the University of Recife, although he became increasingly radical in his outlook after his exile in 1964 (1970, p. 104).

In the early 1960s only less than a third of the adult population of Brazil was eligible to vote. Widespread illiteracy among the rural poor had served the interests of the dominant minority because eligibility for the franchise depended on the ability to read and write.* For this reason, promotion of literacy has tended to be an important part of Brazilian reform movements (Elias 1973, p. 69).

The Catholic Church movement which countered the Peasant Leagues was known as *Movimento de Educacao de Base* (Movement for Basic Education or MEB). de Kadt describes the goals of the movement as he found them in a 1961 document:

---

*In 1985, a new law has eliminated the requirement of literacy for adult franchise.

Basic education, it stated, must confer three benefits on man: a conception of life, making him conscious of his own physical, spiritual, moral, and civic worth; a style of life, which guides behaviour in the personal, family, and social spheres; and finally a mystique of life, which acts as an inner force ensuring dynamism and enthusiasm in the fulfillment of duties and the exercise of rights. Basic education must teach the peasant about the human condition, social behaviour, work, the family, and civic and political organization (1970, pp. 151-52).

These goals became epitomized in the concept of Conscientization, as we shall see later in this chapter.

PAULO FREIRE: BIOGRAPHICAL SKETCH

Paulo Freire was born in Recife in 1921 as the son of a police officer. While still a boy, his father had died. Consequently, and in the wake of the worldwide Depression begun in 1929, Freire and members of his lower middle class family experienced and struggled against poverty and hunger. John L. Elias mentions that during this difficult period:

Freire fell two years behind in his schoolwork. Some of his teachers diagnosed his condition as mental retardation. Freire was deeply affected by this experience of poverty and vowed because of it to work among the poor of the northeast to try to improve their lot (1976, p. 12).

After managing to complete secondary school, Freire studied philosophy and psycho-linguistics as a part-time student at the University of Recife. He also worked as a teacher of Portuguese at a secondary school to help his family. In 1944, he married a schoolteacher, Elza. Just as he has claimed that he learned about loving dialogue from his parents, Freire has asserted that his interest in pedagogy sharpened after his marriage to a teacher. He studied and passed the law examination but did not pursue law as a career. He went to work as a welfare official and later as a director of the Department of Education and Culture of the Ministry of Social Service in the state of Pernambuco. His work brought him into direct contact with the urban poor. From about 1947 he became unhappy about traditional methods of communication with poor people and, particularly about the teaching and learning processes in literacy programs for adults. His concern about the inefficacy of methods for educating illiterate, poor adults was aired in seminars and courses in which he participated at the University of Recife, as it was known at that time. He received his doctorate from that university in history and philosophy of education in 1959 and later became a professor there.

Freire was closely associated with the Movement for Basic Education's (MEB) work to bring about consciousness about democratic rights to the peasants, to break the culture of silence which dependents learn to practice in a "patron-dependent" relationship.* Freire was the director of a program that started in 104 schools in two years for 9,000 children. For adults, he organized radio schools. This interest in adult education was partly influenced by the massive success of the literacy campaign in Cuba in the early 1960s. Freire moved on to become the first director of the University of Recife's Cultural Extension Service in 1962. He started a program in a small area called Angicos in the state of Rio Grande de Norte to teach literacy to poor peasants. Within 45 days, Freire and his team were able to teach 300 peasants and laborers to read and write. This success impressed the state and federal governments, respectively of Arreas and Goulart. A friend of Freire, Paulo de Tarso, had also become Minister of Education in 1962 and had supported Freire. Plans were drawn up to create "culture circles" which would use the Freire method—*Metado Paulo Freire*—to make adults literate. Coordinators were trained by the hundreds in almost every state capital of Brazil.

There was considerable conservative opposition to this whole movement which had been spreading like wildfire. Freire was accused of using the literacy campaign to spread subversive ideas. But the reform-minded Goulart government which had the support of President John F. Kennedy and the Alliance for Progress initiated by him supported the movement.

In early 1964, Goulart and the military began to express open disagreement. Soon, disagreement gave way to conflict. President Lyndon B. Johnson and many of his key advisers and administrators in the State Department and the Central Intelligence Agency supported and encouraged the military takeover. On April 1, 1964, Goulart was overthrown; the military took over the government in a manner reminiscent of the overthrow of Salvador Allende in 1973 in Chile.*

At the time of the coup, Freire was working in Aracaju, capital of the northeast state of Sergipe, with the literacy campaign work-

---

*There is much unnecessary confusion about Freire's relationship with MEB. He did not initiate it; he did not direct it; he was associated with it in his independent role as the first director of the Extension Service of the University of Recife.

*On January 15, 1985 political democracy was re-instated in Brazil.

ers. According to one of the participants, Freire's shipment of slide projectors arrived. The soldiers broke open the boxes, expecting to find machine guns for the violent revolution that Freire was purported to be planning. Although they did not find guns, they arrested Freire who spent 70 days in jail. Here he began his book *Education As The Practice of Freedom,* which he completed in Chile later (Elias 1976, p. 17).

On his release from jail, Freire was stripped of his citizenship. He left, as an exile, for Chile where the Christian Democratic Government, elected in 1964, wanted to use his method to promote participation by the populace in development. President Edwardo Frei of Chile personally supported Freire's method to promote significant agrarian reform. Freire left Chile in 1969 and spent a year at Harvard's Center for Studies in Education and Development and Center for the Study of Development and Social Change. In 1970, he joined the education unit of the World Council of Churches as a consultant. From there, Freire has visited numerous countries including the United States, Canada, Tanzania, India, and Guinea-Bissau, to give assistance to individuals and groups interested in his approach and work.

In 1980, he returned to Brazil, ending 16 years of exile. He is now a professor at the Catholic University of Sao Paulo and is active in the political life of the country. His return and the return of many other intellectuals to Brazil is the result of what was called *abertura* (an opening up) on the part of the Brazilian government, partly in response to President Jimmy Carter's human rights stance.*

It is very difficult to "pigeonhole" Freire. He is a *nordestino* (northerner), a Latin American who has been influenced by the Latin American theories of underdevelopment; he has opposed U.S. theories of modernization which more often than not avoided questions about class struggle and imperialism.

PRELIMINARY EXPLANATION OF CONSCIENTIZATION

How did Freire and his colleagues from Recife manage to help illiterate landless laborers to read and write within 45 days and also "make them critically aware of their own oppressed situation?"

---

*I met Freire for the first time in Brussels. He had come there to receive the first King Baudoin International Development Prize, for which I had nominated him. In Brussels, Freire said to me without any equivocation that he will never again leave Brazil as an exile.

(Mies 1973, p. 1,766). What motivated these landless laborers? Why did they learn with an enthusiasm which they did not evince in traditional government-sponsored programs? To answer these questions, we must understand the concept and process of Conscientization.

The term *conscientizacao* was used widely by Catholic radicals in Brazil in the early 1960s (de Kadt 1970, p. 102). In a talk given in Rome, 1970, Freire explicitly states that he did not invent the term, and credits Bishop Helder Camara for popularizing it and giving it currency in English. Says Freire:

> As soon as I heard it, I realized the profundity of its meaning since I was fully convinced that education, as an exercise in freedom, is an act of knowing, a critical approach to reality (Ladoc 1974, p. 3).

Conscientization respected the dignity of the illiterate adults, began "where they were at," and gave them a sense of confidence about what they could accomplish in this world. Conscientization is the process by which one learns to critically relate oneself and one's work to nature and culture. It enables human beings to reject their status as oppressed objects and achieve their ontological vocation to become subjects. When individuals move from *doxa* (opinion) to *logos* (knowledge), they reach the first level of apprehension for which the French term is *prise de conscience*. Conscientization is the critical development of *prise de conscience* as individuals become involved in the chain of reflection-action-reflection-action. It implies a historical commitment to engage in acts of denouncing oppressors and announcing the liberation of the oppressed so that individuals can, without fear, learn from and teach each other to reshape social reality.

The Freire method rejects the paternalism implicit in most adult literacy programs. It also rejects as paternalistic what Freire refers to as the "banking concept of education" or the "digestive," "nutritionist" approach. Such approaches, says Freire, mystify the process of knowledge creation and knowledge transmission and enable the oppressors to use such mystification to domesticate powerless people. Although it did not start out as such, Conscientization has become a radical theory of political education and action.

Many philosophers and activists, as we have just noted, had contributed to the theory of Conscientization. One of the contributors was the French Christian existentialist Emmanuel Mounier who wrote:

> Liberal democracy has enabled man to become, politically, a subject, but for the most part he remains an object on the plane of economic

existence...[socialism means] the following: The abolition of the proletarian condition; the supersession of the anarchic economy of profit by an economy directed to the fulfillment of the totality of personal needs; the socialization, without state monopoly, of those sectors of industry which otherwise foster economic chaos; the development of co-operative life; the rehabilitation of labour, the promotion, in rejection of all paternalist compromises, of the worker to full personality; the priority of labour over capital; the abolition of class distinctions founded upon the division of labour or of wealth; the priority of personal responsibility over the anonymous organization (1952, pp. 103-4).

We shall refer to Mounier's ideas again in Chapter 4 but may note that Freire (1973a, p. 12) cites him, and de Kadt makes several references to Mounier including the radical Brazilian Catholics' view that the economy must become "a personal economy, of persons and for persons, using means which are appropriate to persons" (1970, p. 67).

Almost everyone who pays homage to education as a progressive force does so because *in the long run* it can be a source and springboard of much goodness in human beings. Conscientization, if carried out, would result in millions of poor people being awakened and, as a result, overthrowing existing power structures and power relations. It is this hope for social change *in the short run* that leads the promoters of Conscientization to emphasize the education of adults, that is, oppressed adults.

Freire and his colleagues would, however, make the case for a continued educational revolution even after the existing power structures are overthrown. The fact that a different group of individuals has taken over political power would not automatically result in the elimination of domination and exploitation, as the case of the Soviet experiment to inaugurate a humane socialist state so clearly shows. The development of a humane society is a long and arduous process; the overthrow of existing power structures can only set the stage for that process to begin. It must be continued through a process committed to education as liberation.

People who have reasonable material security can usually at least take account of the availability of alternative choices to guide their actions. The proponents of Conscientization attempt to develop in people utterly deprived of material security the perception of the possibility of such alternatives. This is done by creating a sense of psychological security which results from the solidarity of the group.

The advocates of Conscientization accept much of the Marxian and neo-Marxian analysis about the need for a dialectical understanding of historical change, the nature of main and secondary contradictions in society arising primarily out of the economic relationships between people, and the necessity for class struggle to bring out real, genuine improvement in the lives of poor people.

The dialectical understanding of history leads Conscientization to take the position that the origins of an individual's concepts of self and self-worth are in his or her relationships with other human beings, and, in a generic sense, with society. The nature of these relationships are significantly influenced by the way human beings create and re-create culture within the constraints imposed by their perceptions of (1) nature (the non-human, material world) and (2) the economic, political, familial, etc. institutions created by human beings since time began. Thus, the world of which one is a part and *in which one has room for action* is neither entirely objective nor entirely subjective. It is *intersubjective*.

We may contrast this view with that of Sarvodaya. According to the ideology of Sarvodaya, the apprehension of the world is primarily a private, personal effort. Other human beings may and do contribute to that knowledge but it is not located in the nature of the relationship between persons. It is formed in one's own mind and soul as a result of one's effort to eliminate ignorance. The position of Conscientization that human beings are essentially differentiated from other, lesser, animate beings by their power to think for themselves and, at least to some extent, to choose courses of action for themselves is grounded in the Greek and later Christian traditions. Sarvodaya acknowledges the importance of the human person but does not assume that human beings have dominion over creation.

The acceptance of the need for class struggle or at least struggle between the oppressed and the oppressors in Conscientization have several programmatic implications of which we shall mention two here. Initially, the process of Conscientization will create in the oppressed people an awareness of personal needs which can only be achieved by changes in the socio-economic system. This initial approach to adaptation and reform will, if rejected by the oppressors, give way to the consciousness of the oppressed as a "class-for-itself" willing to bring about desired changes by violence, if necessary (Barndt 1980, p. 326). Thus, in Conscientization, part of the justification for violent action as a last resort is to help create a social system in which both the oppressed and the oppressors will be liberated: the oppressed from their poverty, ill health, and lack of opportunity for self-development; the oppressors from their existence in golden cages. In Sarvodaya, we may recall, it is relentless psychological pressure—not physical violence—that will liberate the rich as well as the poor.

We shall discuss the pedagogical dimensions of Conscientization in Chapter 6.

CONSCIENTIZATION TODAY

As in the case of Sarvodaya, Conscientization appears—from the vantage point of the mid-1980s—to be a movement that has seen its heyday. Soon after the military coup of 1964, MEB shed its radical orientation. The *communidades de base* (base communities) in Brazil have survived military rule and have again become active, albeit mostly non-violently, in promoting social justice (Bruneau 1980). An attempt to promote Conscientization in Chile was similarly transformed with the death of Salvador Allende in 1973. Nicaragua became a socialist state in 1979 not, mainly, as a result of Conscientization but as the consequence of the determined armed struggle that the Sandinistas waged. Yet, the concept of Conscientization continues to engage the attention of many people.

4

THE RELIGIOUS BASIS OF SARVODAYA AND CONSCIENTIZATION

> But there can be no stranger illusion—and it is an illusion we nearly all share—than this, that because the tools of life are today more specialized and more refined than ever before, that because the technique brought by science is more perfect than anything the world has yet known, it necessarily follows that we are in like degree attaining to a profounder harmony of life, to a deeper and more satisfying culture.
>
> E. Sapir, "Culture, Genuine and Spurious," 1924

Religion may be considered as a recognition on the part of human beings of some higher unseen power or powers as having control over the destiny of the universe, particularly of this world. This higher power (God) is, or powers (gods, or as in the case of Buddhism—which does not subscribe to a belief in God—beings who have achieved perfection) are, seen as being entitled to obedience and reverence. In its collective as well as individual expressions, religion is kept alive, in part, by doctrines that cannot be explained only by resort to rational argument. Out of the belief in these doctrines fortified by faith arise moral imperatives which the adherents follow or fulfill because the unseen God or gods are entitled to obedience and reverence. Conduct and actions are seen as the visible or concrete expression of either the attempts to please God (or the gods) or the outward manifestation of faith. In some instances, both the attempts to please God(s) and the manifestation of faith in God(s) may be constitutive parts of the conduct or the actions.

Ethics, in the sense of a system of customs, mores, and values about human rights and duties, does not necessarily require a religious basis. Ethical principles may sometimes arise from "common sense," that is, from reflections about the relative costs and benefits of various modes of behavior and from glimpses of highly commendable actions by individuals. But, both Sarvodaya and Conscientization in their ethical assertions claim a religious foundation. Hence, it is necessary to explore that foundation.

However, it is essential to avoid two pitfalls. One is the tendency to promote a kind of conceptual imperialism and reductionism. For certain zealots, every thought, word, and deed has a religious basis; or worse, every human thought and action can be reduced to a religious (or anti-religious) motive, precept, or principle. The other pitfall is that of using certain terms with so much elasticity that utter confusion is the inevitable result. In post-independence India, for example, *Satyagraha* has been used in so many different contexts that the word has lost all its denotative effectiveness (Tandon 1980, p. 386).

GOD IS TRUTH

Religious symbols and terms are very familiar to people in countries like India and Brazil. Reformers, more often than not, use them as touchstones and themes to promote change.

A student of Gandhi and Bhave must be alert to the new content they gave to ancient terms and symbols, thereby transforming their meaning. Such transformation of ancient symbols is an essential component of movements for cultural revitalization. Wallace discusses this component as "adaptation":

> In most instances the original doctrine is continuously modified by the prophet, who responds to various criticisms and affirmations by adding to, emphasizing, playing down, and eliminating selected elements of the original visions (1956, pp. 274-75).

Gandhi and Bhave, like Sankaracharya and Vivekananda before them, reinterpreted Hindu scriptures so that they may provide guidance to people faced with new economic, political, and cultural challenges. Reformed Hinduism, Gandhi hoped, would, among other things, stem the challenge Christianity posed through its Western and indigenous missionaries.

Consider the Christian challenge. It emphasized that every human being is a child of God and is therefore worthy of love and respect, in contrast to the Hindu view that individuals are unequal on the basis of the caste into which one is born. Christianity insisted that life on earth is a preparatory and probationary period prior to eternal reward or punishment. The Hindu orientation, on the other hand, required each person to fulfill the rules and regulations of his *jati* so that the operation of the laws of *karma* will ensure a better life in the next incarnation. The effect of this orientation was to make upward social mobility seem an unseen, immutable, intergenerational process which suited extremely well the interests of self-perpetuation of ruling caste groups.

"The great tradition"—as opposed to "the little tradition"—of Hinduism propagates the view that all bona fide religions are like the many paths one can take to reach a mountain top. (On this distinction, see Singer 1972.) These paths, if sincerely and honestly pursued, would lead people to God. This view has led scholars and sages of India, over three millenia, to explain and debate the many ways in which one may seek spiritual salvation. Here, we cannot pause to examine that rich literature. We will, therefore, confine ourselves to Gandhi's and Bhave's views.

Gandhi firmly held the view that there are many paths to God. He also fully subscribed to the *advaita* (non-dualist) *Brahmanist* school of Hinduism which proclaimed that God is but one. He, however, asserted that, in his view, the phrase "God is Love" should be replaced with "God is Truth" (Bondurant 1965, pp. 17-18). Bhave, Gandhi's disciple, also affirms that "Hinduism, Islam and other religions are different formulations of only one basic religion, namely, Truth. And, therefore, though each may have its own peculiarities, there is no opposition between them. One who sees this, really sees" (Bhave 1964, p. 35).

In Chapter 2, we mentioned the dialectical relationship between Sarvodaya and Satyagraha and provided preliminary definitions of both terms. It is now necessary to discuss this relationship in more detail and depth.

Sarvodaya is a way of finding God in the world which, to Gandhi and Bhave, is one essential characteristic of becoming a religious person. It is also a way of experiencing collective *samadhi* (state of ecstacy), namely, recognizing that all creatures on earth are the "kith and kin" of human beings and that unjust differences between them are untruthful (Bhave 1964, pp. 35-37). The Sarvodaya approach takes as its goal the transformation of the human being from preoccupation with egotism to involvement in altruism which will bring true contentment. Satyagraha is the technique that will usher in the new values of Sarvodaya (Sharma 1960). The capacity to see all beings with an equal eye that *samadhi* promotes in individuals cannot admit the identification of groups of oppressors and oppressed. Oppression exists, of course. Desires to oppress others exist in every person because people act on the basis of untruth. Therefore, the appropriate action to bring about necessary social change is to work with everyone—irrespective of ethnicity, class, creed, language, gender, and so on—to seek the truth. The test of the genuine pursuit of truth is that it will bring about changes in personal and social life. An individual who accepts the precepts of Sarvodaya must live according to it. This explains Gandhi's avoidance of attachment to material things and his self-purificatory style of life. Bhave follows in Gandhi's footsteps on the grounds that one's words can have the power of persuasion only to the extent that others perceive one's sincere attempts to live by those words. This personal commitment to an exemplary lifestyle is, perhaps, the most important way one acts to support one's belief. There is an implicit and clear dialectical relationship between faith and action in Gandhi's view: faith leads to truthful action which, in turn, clarifies and strengthens one's faith. While Truth is absolute, human apprehension of it will always be found to be wanting. Says Bhave, "Practice of *Samya-yoga* is the first distinguishing mark of a revolutionary philosophy" (1964, p. 3).

Elaborating on a *Samya-yoga* society, Bhave once explicated its principles on the basis of four verses in the *Bhagavat Gita* (Chap. 4, verses 29-32):

1. No power should be dominant in society; there should only be the discipline of good thought;
2. All faculties of the individual should be dedicated to society which must provide the individual with opportunity for growth and development;
3. The moral, social and economic value of all callings performed honestly should be the same (Ram 1962, p. 471).

Embedded in Satyagraha, one finds several major tenets of Hinduism.* For example, Satyagraha is related to *aparigraha* (the mental and social state of non-attachment to worldly possessions, leading to equanimity), *tapasya* (prolonged, intense contemplation

---

*Gandhi once wrote that "socialism, even communism, is explicit in the first verse of the Ishopanishad" (India, Gov't. of, 1979, Collected Works of Mahatma Gandhi, vol. 64 [Feb. 20, 1937], p. 385). The first verse reads as follows: By Isa is to be covered as this, that which is changeful in the changing world. Hence by renunciation it should be enjoyed. Do not crave for anybody's wealth.

based on self-restraint; acceptance of personal suffering that leads to spiritual autonomy and inner peace) and may be contrasted to *duragraha* (the persistent desire for self-aggrandizement, the result of which is wrongdoing). In view of the focus of this book on Sarvodaya as a social movement, we need to emphasize only three tenets—*ahimsa, karmayoga,* and *dharma*—which have more direct social relevance than, for instance, *tapasya* or *ahankara* (egotistical self-love) or *moksha* (salvation).

Ahimsa, to begin with, simply means the conscious renunciation of the desire to harm, or more specifically, to kill any animate thing. Gandhi, however, emphasized that *ahimsa* must include the dictum of "love thine enemy." If such love is genuine, it would lead to an experience of conversion which obliterates the adversarial relationship between two or more individuals or groups and raise them to a higher level of action and aspiration.

The two constituent terms of *karmayoga* are words which are now almost part of the English language: karma (the view that a person shall reap as he or she sows, to some extent in this life but also in future incarnations) and yoga (a disciplined, ascetic way of subjugating and tuning the body and the mind to achieve a state of spiritual "steadystate" or "bliss"). Iyer refers to *karmayoga* as a process of self-purification connected to the service of suffering humanity (1973, p. 49). A *karmayogi* chooses to act, to be involved, with faith in the perfectibility of persons, in the improvement of earthly life on the basis of meditation and personal suffering. She or he chooses not to make an ascetic life—the life of a *sanyasi*—an end in itself. Although Gandhi respected *jnana* (knowledge) *yoga* and *bhakti* (devotional) *yoga* as also ways of seeking blissful union with God, he preferred for himself and recommended to others *karmayoga.* Obsession with personal salvation, said Gandhi, could be a display of selfishness. He might have recognized that obsession with *varnashramadharma* (performance of caste obligations, rituals, etc.) to assure oneself a better next birth would not motivate people to act individually and collectively to improve matters in this life.* Prayerful meditation and personal suffering should produce in a human being, on the one hand, a sense of dedication to his or her worldly cause and, on the other, *nishkamakarma,* "a deliberate attitude of detachment from the fruits of actions" (Iyer 1973, p. 236).

---

*Indeed, many commentators have asserted that a revolution of the kind that took place in China (culminating in the proclamation of the People's Republic in 1949) would not occur in India as long as belief in reincarnation is widespread.

Dharma, among other things, refers to the obligation a *karmayogi* must sense to take actions in one's relationship to others which would enhance the welfare of all. In proclaiming a pro-active view of *dharma,* Gandhi eschewed the reactive view which equated dharma with mere observance of caste ceremonies, rules, and precedents. Gandhi's writings sometimes equate *dharma* with rather vague phrases like "the moral law of the universe," "the natural law," "the cosmic principle," "Absolute Truth," etc. One can only surmise that he means by them the essential principles of *ahimsa* and the universal commandment, "Do unto others as you would have them do unto you."

The Sarvodaya approach partakes of a deeply Hindu outlook which claims that the soul (*atman*) is the Godhead in human beings and it "partakes of the ultimate reality (brahman)" (Sharma 1960, p. 259). The soul is unable to achieve unity with God because of ignorance (*avidya*). One implication of this view is that human beings are innately good and that, despite their ignorance, they can strive to shed the evil personality or behavior which have become habitual with them. Thus, in Sarvodaya, as in Hinduism, religion becomes the pursuit of perfection, the search for the acquisition of Godlike qualities.

How does a *karmayogi* who wants to bring about Sarvodaya—the rising of all—practice dharma? Any abstract theory or exhortation usually carries with it pragmatic injunctions for implementation. This is true of Sarvodaya as well. For example, one would ascertain the facts of a situation as objectively as possible and apply the theory or the principles in context. One should be ready to make tactical concessions if they do not affect the fundamental principles. However, a satyagrahi involved in Sarvodaya is enjoined not to win arguments but to go beyond argument to achieve reconciliation. It is absolutely essential that a person who sees himself as an enemy of the Sarvodaya movement today is dealt with in such a way that tomorrow he or she may be transformed into a friend. How does one do this?

Power has been defined as the ability of X to influence the behavior of Y (X and Y could be one or more persons) without substantially modifying X's own behavior. Power can be exercised in three ways: *normative,* that is, by X appealing to Y to change Y's behavior on the basis of shared assumptions and values; *remunerative,* that is, by X offering to Y something in return for Y's compliance; and, *coercive,* that is, by X threatening to punish or punishing Y to secure compliance. The satyagrahi is absolutely forbidden to use coercion since it will run counter to the principle of *ahimsa.* The satyagrahi, as X, has recourse to persuasion in two major ways: by communicating with Y and by living the kind of life which will be persuasive to Y. (By definition, Y cannot be, in a particular instance, a satyagrahi; otherwise there would have been no call on X to confront Y.) But, what if persuasion of this kind fails? Then the satyagrahi can undertake a series of penances which would cause physical suffering to his or her own being. These acts may put tremendous pressure on Y, and bring forth the innate good "instincts" of Y which, in turn, may lead to the modification of Y's behavior. Certain critics of Gandhi have suggested that this is coercion too because it is psychological violence. Gandhi had, however, always insisted that penitential imposition of suffering on oneself is not merely a manipulative device. X is also praying and meditating, ceaselessly questioning his or her own motives and behavior so that when X and Y meet in humility, each forgives the other, learns from the other, and enriches the other spiritually. Thus, the eventual reconciliation leaves no bitter aftertaste. This was what Gandhi meant by "purity of means." The "pure means" eliminate the need for Y to look for another occasion to "settle the score" because both X and Y have, as it were, won.

The principle of *aparigraha* (non-attachment to material possessions) is another important foundation of Sarvodaya. In Sarvodaya, to use a cliché, people are more important than things. A sanyasi can practice *aparigraha* in an extreme form by literally not owning any material things (other than a piece of cloth to cover his or her nakedness). A *karmayogi* cannot take that choice because of his involvement in the world. The Sarvodaya movement, therefore, has deduced four principles from the tenet of *aparigraha*. These principles relate to work because it is in work that people deal directly with material things to cooperate with and in some instances transform nature.

1. Opportunities to work with things ought to enable people to use and develop their abilities.
2. Such work should assist people to minimize their ego-centeredness and to maximize opportunities to work with others for improving the welfare of all.
3. Everyone ought to be directly involved in making or growing at least some of the things he or she needs for sustenance. Then, no one will be so heavily involved in manual labor that they do not have time to develop their mental and spiritual potential which would be an immoral state of affairs.

4. The primary criterion for producing goods and services should be the enhancement of the quality of life for all and not the relentless pursuit of profit by the few.

Since Sarvodaya as a social movement came into existence in India, it is appropriate to ask about its stance on the caste system which has been one of the universal foundations of Indian society. Gandhi accepted the fourfold division of society and the four divisions of life (*Varnashrama dharma*) but was against the evils the caste system had perpetrated in Indian society (Narayan 1969, pp. 473-80). Bhave, however, was not content to denounce the evils of the caste system; he denounced the entire system as an aberration. In so doing, Bhave had questioned an essential part of the Hindu *weltanschauung* which claimed that human beings are at birth unequal and that the inequality is the result of their actions in previous births which justifies differential access to wealth, power, and enjoyment in their contemporary life.

Hinduism, unlike Christianity, does not have a set of codified doctrines, a carefully developed bureaucratic hierarchy, and a cadre of priests who have pastoral responsibilities. It is much more "a way of life" than a religion. Baptism, heresy, and excommunication do not exist in Hinduism.* Its genius is in its ability to be responsive to local needs. This feature of Hinduism is accurately reflected in Sarvodaya's preference for decentralization of power and the development of more or less autonomous village republics.

The worth of a civilization, according to the principles of Sarvodaya, is not measured by the glory of its material possessions, martial prowess, or technological advancement but by its willingness to use material possessions mainly to promote spiritual regeneration and personal fulfillment among individuals and communal harmony within society.

WE ARE ALL CHILDREN OF GOD

It would be highly presumptuous for anyone—especially one who has not devoted years of study to this topic—to try to explicate the Biblical basis, augmented by 19 centuries of scholarship, of doing theological and pastoral work in situations in which people

---

*A Westerner came to Kerala, India in my student days and requested the *pujaris* (priests) in a temple to baptize him to Hinduism according to the proper rites. He was disappointed to find out that no baptismal ceremony existed.

were struggling for liberation from economic, political, and cultural oppression. All that one can do is to recapitulate a few general premises in this section that would serve as a "curtain raiser" to the more specific discussion of Catholic radicalism in Brazil.

The starting points of liberation theology, perhaps, are the Biblical claims that all human beings are the children of God and are equal in the eyes of God; all of the earth and the resources ("fruits") in it are for the use and enjoyment of God's children.* The relationship human beings have with God, however, is not confined to use and enjoyment. They have an active and continuing responsibility to work in history, as God's partners, to continue the work of humane creation. Yet, in all areas of the earth including ancient Israel, there was (and still is) misery and poverty because people did not obey God's commandments and had "hardened their hearts" against Him. The presence of evil in the world must be acknowledged by God's children; they must fight against it so that justice may prevail.

Here we arrive at a very difficult issue, namely, the relationship of faith in Christ to works, that is, what Christians as individuals and groups must do. There are those who would argue that the expression of faith must always be by individuals as individuals and that Christians as a group have no right to arrogate to themselves the responsibility for creating God's kingdom on earth. That responsibility belongs not to mere mortals but to Jesus Christ when He returns again at His appointed time (the "Second Coming"). They would maintain that the salvation of human beings was wrought by God when He willingly sent His son Jesus Christ to the world to save sinners; He died to atone for the sins of the world which came into existence with Adam's original sin. According to this strict interpretation of the doctrine of salvation through grace, human beings cannot do good deeds and thus ingratiate themselves into the grace of God. However, Christians can and must express their faith—that is, the personal, voluntary commitment they make to accept Jesus Christ as their savior—in their worldly life, so that uncommitted Christians and others may discern Christlike qualities in Christians, much as we discern the goodness of a tree by its fruit. Some Christians, like some Hindus, have seen in the life of Jesus non-attachment to material things and desires and have lived in great simplicity in monasteries or among the people.

---

*We cannot, of course, explore here the sociologically constrained interpretations of these claims in different times and places.

Christians who are committed to Conscientization do not necessarily or directly question the doctrine of salvation through grace. But they make two emendations: God's work in the world must be done by human beings and we are therefore enjoined to struggle against evil not only in its manifestations in persons but also in society. They would point to Jesus' summation of all the commandments, namely, to love God and to love one's neighbor, the denunciation of oppression by prophets such as Isaiah, Jeremiah, and Amos in the Old Testament who spoke without fear against the way many social institutions functioned to deprive human beings of their rightful share of God's earth and of their God-given right to develop themselves mentally and spiritually. Spokesmen for this type of "Liberation Theology" use the book of Exodus, the prophetic-tradition in the Old Testament, the Old Testament assertion that to know God (Yahweh) is to do justice, events in the life of Jesus, and the writings of St. Thomas Aquinas and others to denounce the existence of poor people by the side of rich people. They assert that Christ is on the side of the oppressed people.

Some liberation theologians who support Conscientization are prepared to see Jesus in some respects as a time-bound figure whose eternally valid message must be reinterpreted for our time. This stance leads them to understand oppression, morality, liberation, and immorality in terms of the cultural milieu of particular societies.

CATHOLIC RADICALISM IN BRAZIL

Brazil is a Roman Catholic nation; the Roman Catholic Church in Brazil is the largest in the world. Institutional Catholicism—94 percent of all Brazilians claim to be Roman Catholics—is as much a part of Brazilian social life as Hinduism is a part of Indian life.

Although "the discovery and settlement of Brazil was a joint venture of the Portuguese state and the Catholic Church" (Bruneau 1974, p. 12), church-state relations have been close (involving the domination of the church by the state) during some periods and distant during other periods of Brazil's five centuries of history. During the 1950s and early 1960s, the Catholic Church's influence had waned in considerable measure. Bruneau in his study of the Brazilian Catholic Church as a social institution argues that the promotion of social change was the church's new approach to retaining or regaining influence in Brazilian society. What interests us, however, is the religious grounds on which the church based its support of Conscientization. These arguments were significantly influenced by two encyclicals, *Mater et Magistra* (1961) and *Pacem in Terris* (1963) of Pope John XXIII which attempted to put the Catholic Church definitely on a progressive, as opposed to traditional, course in human history.

de Kadt points out that at the 1959 council of the students' branch of the loosely federated Catholic Action named *Juventude Universitaria Catolica* a Catholic priest named Almery presented a paper that was highly influential. In it, says de Kadt, Almery suggested that it

> is not sufficient to know that they have a task to fulfill in this world, a task which would involve such matters as "creating a Christian social order", "bringing salvation to the social structures", or "restoring all things to Christ"....Though a Christian will find the *ultimate* meaning of history in his faith, faith is not necessarily of any help in enabling him to make sense out of the history of his own time and society. On the one hand the teaching of the church and the speculations of theologians have provided him with the universal principles by which to guide his action. Social scientists, on the other hand, have supplied many facts and some theories about society, but these facts and theories are usually not connected with an explicit philosophical, let alone, theological, concern. [Padre] Almery therefore concluded that:
>
>> it is absolutely necessary, if we aim at an effective Christian commitment in the temporal order, to reflect amply and carefully in the light of reality...so that we may arrive at certain *principia media* [intermediate principles] which express what one might call a Christian historical ideal.
>
> He added, however, that knowledge and reflection by themselves are not enough for the emergence of such intermediate principles; reality must also be experienced personally, by living in it actively and with commitment (de Kadt 1970, p. 63).

This extensive quote ought to familiarize us with the basic orientation of those who wished to move the church toward involvement in socio-political change as a prelude to bringing about a more humane Christian society. In Chapter 7 we shall discuss some aspects of the attempts to implement the intermediate Christian historical ideal. It is, however, necessary here to accord some recognition to one of the progressive bishops, Dom Helder Camara, who articulated the progressive Brazilian Roman Catholic position. In *Revolution Through Peace* (1971) he wrote:

Our obligation is to serve; it is our human Christian duty to help lead the Children of God out of the subhuman state in which they live. Misery degrades human life and is an outrage to the Creator and Father.

When the church proclaims, as it did in Mar del Plata, that the socioeconomic structures of this continent are unjust and in urgent need of rapid and radical reform, it is not with the intention of evading our share of responsibility for the deplorable situation Latin America is in today; as the supreme spiritual force of the Christian continent, we could and should have done our part to bring about a far more just and humane state of things (p. 105).

As human beings and Christians, we cannot but thrill to the idea of progress. God made us in His own image, and He is not a petty, jealous God. Having entrusted man with finishing the work of Creation, He feels a Father's thrill of pride at seeing His Steward splitting the atom, sprinkling the sky with stars, and mastering nature.

And yet human selfishness makes of progress a cruel thing. For instance, automation in developed countries makes more people jobless every month, though industry—if not that of peace, then that of war—absorbs the unemployed victims of the electronic and cybernetic age (p. 116).

We have even witnessed the absurdity of seeing one of the most beautiful expressions of the democratic vocabulary—*conscientizacao*—condemned as a word that, if not actually red, was certainly tinged with pink. What could be more democratic than awakening a numbed consciousness, which implies goading a man's intelligence and encouraging his sense of freedom, two of the highest gifts bestowed on man by God? (p. 133).

If Camara is a pacifist revolutionary, Freire is a revolutionary who believes that the need for violence at certain moments in history to bring about social transformation must not be avoided.

Freire confesses that he is not a theologian "but merely an onlooker intrigued by theology, which has indelibly marked...my pedagogy...." (Ladoc 1974, p. 14). Freire's talks and writings contain many references and allusions to Jesus Christ, the Bible, St. Thomas Aquinas, and contemporary writers such as Reinhold Niebuhr, Teilhard de Chardin, and Paul Tillich. His early work in Pernambuco had the support of Dom Helder Camara.

Freire never says he is a Christian. He will only admit to "trying to become a Christian." That statement makes him, in some ways, a Hindu because, according to the Christian doctrine of salvation through grace, one cannot "try to become a Christian." In Hinduism, on the other hand, it is possible—indeed very desirable—to try to become more holy. Freire does not deal with the doctrine "original sin" and accepts the Marxian view that human character is formed as a consequence of the complex interaction of individuals with each other and with nature. Thus, Freire's understanding of the nature of ethics and morality contains a relativistic dimension that is in some ways similar to the Hindu view. Freire also said in the course of a talk in Australia in 1974 that he met Christ when he was a boy; he met Marx as an adult working with poor people. On another occasion he said: "Christ led me to the people, the people led me to Marx." The following excerpts are taken from a letter Freire wrote to a doctoral candidate in theology:

> I am convinced that we as Christians have an enormous task to perform, presuming that we are capable of setting aside our idealistic myths and in that way sharing in the revolutionary transformation of society, instead of stubbornly denying the extremely important contribution of Karl Marx. Being a Christian does not necessarily mean being a reactionary; and in the same way, being a Marxist does not necessarily mean being a dehumanizing bureaucrat.... Never, perhaps, have we needed a theological rebirth as much as today.
> This, it seems to me, must be the primary concern for the theologians of the Third World: to be men of that World. But being a man of the Third World also means siding with the oppressed, with the condemned of the earth, in a posture of authentic love that cannot possibly straddle both camps. The greatest, in fact the only proof of true love that the oppressed can show their oppressors is not to bend, masochistically, to their oppression but to take away from them, radically, those objective conditions that make it possible for them to oppress. Only in that way can the oppressors be humanized. And this loving task, which is both political and revolutionary, devolves on the oppressed themselves. Oppressors, the oppressing class, can never liberate others, nor can they liberate themselves either.
> Only the weakness of the oppressed is strong enough to do that. A daring theology of revolution must grasp this distinction and go far beyond St. Thomas in recognizing the right to rebellion. So too, a theology of violence has to unmask a series of myths—for example, that only the oppressed person is violent, as he defends himself from the violence of his oppressor. The violence of the oppressed is not really violence at all, but a legitimate reaction: it is an affirmation of one who no longer fears freedom, who knows that it is not a gift but a conquest (LADOC 1974, pp. 11-12; 14).

Since the primary purpose of this book is the comparison of two ethical philosophies, we may take special note of the importance of

Emmanuel Mounier's personalist philosophy on radical Catholicism in Brazil.

That Mounier was influential is attested by de Kadt, Bruneau, and Freire; we are not in a position to gauge the extent of the influence. What does interest us is Mounier's attempt, particularly in his post-World War II writings, to promote Christian-Marxist dialogue and thus find a third way between capitalism and communism, in many ways similar to Sarvodaya's quest. In the first issue of *Espirit* in 1932 Mounier wrote:

> We say: Primacy of the spiritual.... On the Right they are trying hard to weld together the bloc: property-family-country-religion.... Most of the new forces, in contrast are on the Left.
>
> Our final goal is not the happiness, the comfort, the prosperity of the city, but the spiritual flowering of man.... Marxism is...the concrete representation of our deficiency. We must join to it a philosophy of our own fabrication. We will work at doing that.
>
> We are...revolutionaries, but in the name of the spirit.
>
> It is not force which makes revolutions, it is light.
>
> A first abstract humanism was constituted in the Renaissance, dominated by the mystique of the individual; a second humanism every bit as abstract and no less inhuman is being constituted today in the USSR, dominated by the collectivist mystique. The gigantic struggle which is taking shape before our eyes...opposes the first Renaissance which is collapsing to the second which is in preparation. The tragedy of the battle is that man is in two camps, and if one destroys the other, he loses an integral part of himself.
>
> The West defends structure, the East, communion. We must certainly integrate the two (Hellman 1981, p. 53).

Mounier considered it an urgent necessity to propose a society of persons, for persons, and by persons. The priority, he wrote, had to be "personal responsibility over the anonymous organization" (1952, p. 104). These ideas appear to echo at first blush Gandhi's and Bhave's proposals for self-contained village republics. Whether they do will be the subject of later discussion.

The religious bases of Sarvodaya and Conscientization, as described in this chapter, appear to be syncretic. Hinduism—without a bureaucratic organization, codified doctrines, or a carefully trained cadre of priests who must submit to a hierarchy of authority—has always been susceptible to syncretism. We now recognize that Catholicism too is susceptible to syncretic tendencies, to mix principles that can be joined only with considerable intellectual ingenuity, indeed verbal pyrotechnics. For example, Dewitt raises the question of how Freire can maintain that human beings are radically free to be and at the same time accept a dialectical explanation of change in society (1971, pp. 183-87). The result of such syncretism, however, has been the development of radical Christianity and radical Hinduism, as one of the bases for promoting cultural revitalization in, respectively, Brazil and India.

5

THE CHALLENGES OF MARXISM AND NATIONALISM

On the cover of *Christians in the Nicaraguan Revolution* is the photograph of a young girl (Randall 1983). A rather large wooden cross on a coarse string adorns her bosom; her blouse is a typical military shirt—there are two pens in one of the pockets. A rifle slung over her right shoulder juts from the back. But it is her face that is riveting. It suggests a confusion of emotions: sorrow, anger, fear, and hope. These same emotions are very much present in the responses Sarvodaya and Conscientization as social movements make to the challenges of Marxism and nationalism.

We have already noted that both Sarvodaya and Conscientization are attempts to face squarely the misery of billions of human beings on earth; to respond creatively to the structures that constrain efforts to develop policies and practices that will enable people to develop their full potential as physical and spiritual beings. They oppose the extreme, unfair inequalities of wealth and access to resources that industrialization has brought about. They, although to different degrees, see the state as an inherently oppressive social institution. They recognize the critically important role in society of peasants, industrial workers, and a host of others who do physical labor; they share an abhorrence for the rules of the societal game that keep manual laborers at the lowest rungs of prestige. They proclaim the necessity for a revolution, for a fundamental transformation of social relations.

One conviction drives them: human beings and human society can eventually be far more just than they are. Sarvodaya and Conscientization oppose the utilitarian principle that social policies must attempt to ensure the greatest good of the greatest number. They assert that any just society must ensure the good of all. They are prophetic in their denunciations as well as their vision. The adherents of Sarvodaya and Conscientization are aware of the revolutionary movements of earlier times which have been betrayed or coopted so that exploitation and unjust inequalities have persisted, even exacerbated.

All variants of Marxism share the characteristics of Sarvodaya and Conscientization outlined above. Let us explore the similarities and differences in greater detail.

SARVODAYA AND MARXISM

One discovers in the course of examining the literature that there is a veritable cottage industry of scholarship contrasting Gandhians and Marxists. This section cannot possibly add much to that literature. What we can profitably do is summarize it to advance the comparison of Sarvodaya and Conscientization.

A brief historical excursion: Mookerjee mentions that "It is also held by some that Feurbach's anti-Christian materialism, which led to Marxism...was originally inspired by his studies of Indian Philosophy...if one accepts the view that the single great influence on Karl Marx was Hegel, it can be said that Marxism also contained, at least in its dialectics, the essential attributes of Indian thinking" (1967, p. 13). The reference here, of course, is to the *advaita* view that everything in the universe is rooted in Brahma and thus all beings—human and non-human—are connected to each other by their common bond to Brahma.

There is some small basis for claims such as: "Gandhism is Communism minus violence"; "Gandhism is Communism plus God";-or, "Marxism is Sarvodaya minus God." Bhave in 1951 referred to Gandhi as the great soul (mahatma) and called Marx the great thinker (mahamani) (Mashruwala 1951, p. 15). Yet, serious scholars have eschewed facile generalizations because the differences between Gandhism and Marxism are fundamental.

Belief in God is a fundamental point of departure for Sarvodaya. There is a divine spark in all human beings because they all have *atma* (soul) which is God's presence in every person. It is to this divine or higher aspect in human beings that Sarvodaya appeals for the improvement of the person and the just reconstruction of society. All individuals—irrespective of their race, ethnicity, religion, age, gender, social class, or physical disability—have the divine spark in them, although ignorance makes them selfish and greedy. They can all be persuaded to work together. It is out of this assertion about the fundamental divinity of human beings that

Hinduism requires everyone to practice *sadharanadharma* (the duty of everyone to all other persons).

Marx's view of religion as the opiate of the people was grounded in a dialectical materialist view of the world which did not need a creating, regulating, and judging God.

Gandhi's emphasis on God did not lead him to take a private, pietistic, and mystical attitude toward the world. He had the attitude of a scientist which is explicit in the subtitle of his autobiography, "The Story of *My Experiments* with Truth" (Gandhi 1940; italics added). The techniques of Satyagraha were developed in the crucible of experience, of trials and errors. Gandhi thus shares with Marx at least a few of the attitudes of a scientist, although the Gandhian principles of *ahimsa, satyagraha,* and *sarvodaya* are opposed to the dialectical materialist principles of class-based action.

We may briefly remark on one outcome of this opposition. Marx and Engels were sure that they had found the basic scientific laws that govern human society. Therefore, they were quite hopeful about the eventual arrival of a classless society. Gandhi was far less sure. True, he proposed a vision of India as a loosely federated group of more or less autonomous village republics. But, it was a statement of preference. For Gandhi, far more than for Marx and Engels, the future was open for construction or destruction (Mashruwala 1951, pp. 87–88).

The Gandhian respect for manual laborers is similar to the Marxian respect for the proletariat. There is in both Sarvodaya and Marxism a sense of outrage that a small group of individuals lives luxuriously off the backs of a large group of toilers. Both Gandhi and Marx envisioned the possibility of everyone participating in socially necessary productive labor thus ensuring for everyone leisure with which to enjoy life and develop oneself. Yet, there are two crucial differences between the Gandhian and Marxian approaches. In Gandhi's vision of self-governing village republics, there is an unmistakable yearning to recapture a "golden age," a mythical past when Rama, a Hindu God, ruled and all was well with the world in *Ramraj.* Marx, however, shared with his European contemporaries a belief in the inevitability of human progress. Gandhi's acceptance of karma and reincarnation is a fundamentally cyclical notion in contrast to the implication of linearity in theories of human progress. (The Hindu cyclical view of life in the universe is represented by a symbol which, due to its misappropriation as the swastika by the Nazis in the 1930s, has become odious to many people.) Second, Marx's defense of the proletariat is grounded in a carefully constructed theoretical apparatus based on the generation of surplus value in production; hence his and Engel's claim that they are scientific socialists. Gandhi's love for the poor people, like that of the prophets of ancient Israel, is based on moral and religious grounds.

For the Marxists, the concept of class denotes the empirically demonstrable fact of groups of people either dominating or being dominated by other people on the basis of whether they own and control the means of production. The human being is distinguished from all other beings by virtue of the fact that by manual and mental labor they transform nature and in the process create culture. Any attempt to systematically and scientifically understand society must clarify the role that work plays in the natural world and in the relationships of people. Class, to the Marxists, depicts the place a person or a group of persons occupy in the process of work, that is, the production of goods and services which ensure a society's continued existence. What is unscientific (and unjust) about all previous and current societies—but particularly capitalist society—is that those who produce wealth (the workers) are exploited by those who do not, because the latter own and control the means by which wealth is produced. This fact enables the bourgeoisie to retain the surplus value that workers produce. Class, however, is not a static phenomenon. Those who, historically, have come to occupy the position of owning and controlling the means of production ensure their continued dominance not only by expropriating the surplus value that workers produce but also by controlling institutions such as the state, the judiciary, the media, and education so that the ruling ideas and practices will keep the producers of wealth in a relationship of exploitation and domination. In contrast, the Sarvodaya view about social divisions is much closer to Max Weber's notion of social class, namely, the pattern of life chances for individuals resulting from the complex interaction of status positions, in which economic status is an extremely important but not determining factor.

To the Marxists, moral laws are not given—inscribed on stone tablets or otherwise—to human beings by God but are the products of the complex interaction of the non-human world, culture (which includes technical change) and human beings (some of whom are exploiters). This position led Marx to locate the force for human progress in our times in a class of human beings, the proletariat. They would overthrow another class, the bourgeoisie and establish a classless society, following an era of "the dictatorship of the proletariat."

In Sarvodaya, the enemy is within each of us; the attitude is one of *anaasakti* (non-attachment) which Bhave claimed was opposed to the Marxist attitude of *aasakti* (attachment) (Mashruwala 1951, p. 17). Sarvodaya, thus, prohibits *the relentless pursuit of power,* even to serve people. The Sarvodaya approach to the development of the person and the society is based on the conscious regulation and limitation of material wants in individuals. This stance is in sharp contrast to the Marxian (and generally Western) view which promotes the proliferation of wants as a *sine qua non* promoting economic growth leading to development.

Nothing else marks Sarvodaya as a truly indigenous Indian movement as the premise of the desirability of non-attachment. Attachment is understandable, even necessary, in, for example, the *Grahasthasrama* (homemaker) stage in a person's life and to meet essential needs of social survival and community development. However, one must strive to develop and promote an attitude of non-attachment to material things. The principal tenets of Sarvodaya include respect for the individual but the individual is seen in the context of the community in a way that is reminiscent of the Marxist emphasis on the social nature of the development of persons. But Sarvodaya rejects the classical liberal view of the individual propounded by Thomas Hobbes and John Locke. To them, individuality is, in part, affirmed by a person's right to have and dispose of property (Mukherjee 1979, p. 403). Marxism shares with classical liberalism the view that the person is the "absolute, natural proprietor of [one's] own capacities" (Mukherjee 1979, p. 403). There is no such assertion in Sarvodaya writings. In Sarvodaya, unlike in Marxism, private property is permitted provided that the holders of it see it as a "trust" with which they can serve the community. Here, again, we see the importance of the principles of disinterested service and non-attachment.

Sarvodaya, too, wants a revolution but it must be by agreement, not violence. The proponents of Sarvodaya recognize that a revolution by agreement will take long to bring about but insist that the effects will last longer. Let us also note that using psychological pressure to persuade recalcitrant individuals and groups is permissible, indeed recommended. The Sarvodaya ideologists will point to the disappointment of Marxist revolutionaries who discovered that no New Jersualem awaited them in the morning after their seizure of power as evidence of the ineffectiveness of violent revolution. They will point also to the records of post-revolutionary societies such as the Soviet Union, Israel, China, Cuba, and Vietnam to buttress their argument that violent revolutions do not solve the real problems of poverty and oppression or create emancipatory institutions.

Sarvodaya and Marxism are in agreement about the existence

and importance of conflict in society. Their disagreement, however, about how to approach conflict is profound.

Gandhi insisted that the technique of Satyagraha prohibits the use of physical violence. Non-violence, however, is a brave response to injustice. Gandhi emphasized the need for courage by saying categorically "When there is only a choice between cowardice and violence, I would advise violence" (Mukherjee 1979, p. 407). Satyagraha also proclaims the need for passive resistance on a massive scale to confront unjust social institutions and practices.

The prohibition against violence is usually justified by reference to means and ends. To reach a good goal one's means must be good also. Violent means cannot lead to a just society. Bhave was sarcastic in his characterization of the communist vision: "There will be first rivers of blood, then rivers of milk and honey, and then will follow those of fresh and cool water flowing by each happy home assuaging the thirst of all mankind" (Mashruwala 1951, p. 19).

Moreover, a goal, by definition, is in the future which one cannot, in the last analysis, control. Means, however, are in the present and are subject to our control (Mookherji 1961, p. 226). The proponents of Sarvodaya argue that the means under our control must be good to ensure that the goal will also be good. Then, the conflict-ridden situation can be transformed into a situation where love and truth prevail.

The Marxist response to the Sarvodaya prescription of "pure means for pure goals" is well known. It is unfair to the Marxists to say that they advocate violence as a matter of course. Their advocacy of violence is advanced on the grounds of realism: when persuasion fails, power can deliver. Marxists characterize as a naive travesty of historical experience the view that people who derive disproportionate benefits from a particular socio-economic arrangement will willingly give up those benefits as a result of moral suasion. They will do so only when forced to do so, if necessary with violent confrontation. The "pure means" proposed by Gandhi and Bhave is totally ineffective, say the Marxists, against the impure means of structural violence that perpetuate injustice. The Gandhians respond by pointing to the effectiveness of passive resistance on the basis that the perpetrators of injustice need the cooperation of the oppressed to stay in power; withdrawal of the cooperation will ensure that the oppressors would fall like a house of cards pushed by a little finger. Das Gupta has rightly accused the post-Gandhi sarvodayites of ignoring passive resistance and emphasizing trusteeship. Recent neo-Marxist scholarship, however, has shown that the cooperation of the poor, oppressed people is based not just on false consciousness built on centuries of indoctrination but also on realistic calculations of short-run costs and benefits. The preaching of unctous rectitude does not, say the Marxists, address such complex motivations. But the Sarvodaya proponents can respond with equal vigor that Marxists have no effective way to deal with the problem either.

It would be instructive to examine one item of empirical evidence in this connection. Sachchidananda et al. (1976) have provided us with the results of an excellent study of the dilemmas posed by movements professing revolutionary goals. The Musahari Community Development Block of the district of Muzaffarpur in north Bihar was the locale of the study. This area was one of the strongholds of Naxalities in 1969 and 1970. The Naxalities were a relatively small group of Maoists who had decided to undertake direct, violent acts against landlords and other exploiters of poor people in different parts of India, particularly in the states in West Bengal and Bihar. Their decision and actions were, they claimed, a response to the continuation and exacerbation of misery in the rural areas in independent India and the apparent inability of the Communist Party of India to organize the masses to oppose the capitalist state and system. They hoped that they could develop a peasant movement in India essentially similar to Mao's efforts in the 1930s that culminated in the proclamation of a People's Republic in China. The Naxalite movement was effectively and ruthlessly snuffed out by Indian police action by 1970.

A group of Sarvodaya workers initiated an attempt to bring about a peaceful transformation in Musahari. They hoped that "the challenge of violence could be used to speed up the process of nonviolent social change and reconstruction that Vinobaji had initiated through his Gramdan-Gramswaraj movement" (Narayan, quoted in Sachchidananda 1976, p. 7).

Using questionnaires and interview schedules, the authors of the study collected data from people in 15 villages. Information on the extent to which people participated in decision making, restoration of social rights to Harijans (ex-untouchables), the quality of Sarvodaya leadership, benefits of *Gramdan,* and so on are presented in their report.

The study concluded that four years (1970 to 1974) of Sarvodaya work had yielded some positive results in increasing people's self-esteem and reducing gross and crude exploitation. But, the major conclusion was that the Sarvodaya movement was unable "to transform its initial success into substantive change in [the] socio-economic life of the people" (Sachchidananda 1976, p. 54). Even more depressing conclusions followed. Nothing was or could be done to solve the problem of uneven land distribution. The leadership lacked charismatic qualities and could not effectively prevent the formation of factions and the eruption of infighting. The Sarvodaya movement, by providing some relief to the existing system, strengthened rather than weakened the semi-feudal bondage of poor landless laborers to the dominant castes that owned the land. The movement was taken over by relatively well-to-do people who only wanted to make minor changes to the system. One major conclusion of the study stated:

> What the movement needs is, in order to become a mass movement, to incorporate those who really need a radical change and restructuring, *viz*, the landless people. If the movement is for them, then let it be *their movement,* even if it means leaving the present set of *Sarvodaya* workers out (Sachchidananda 1976, p. 79; italics in the original).

The conclusions of this study are not, perhaps, surprising. The implications will be discussed in Chapter 8.

SARVODAYA AND ANARCHISM

Adi H. Doctor in his excellent study *Anarchist Thought in India* (1964) has argued persuasively that it is very difficult to trace Gandhi's and Bhave's anarchist ideas to ancient Hindu writings on politics. Ostergaard and Currell agree but point to the ancient principle of *ahimsa* which Gandhi transformed from "an ethical principle for the self-realization of the *individual*" to "a principle of *social* ethics and [insisted] on its application, as far as possible, to all social relations" (1971, p. 30; italics in the original). Hinduism, as we have already noted, is a way of life and not an organized religion; it does not have a pyramidic organizational structure or a pope or codified doctrines which, on acceptance, lead to one's salvation. The practice of Hinduism is very much a personal and local phenomenon. No national or international organization attempts to promote proselytization or keep the adherents in line. This ethos of Hinduism is akin to the anarchist ethos.

Sarvodaya and Marxism share a vision of an *ultimate goal:* the withering away of the state. Western anarchism is the logical but extreme extension of the classical liberal position regarding the inviolability of every individual. The notion that "property is theft" arises because the right of some persons to have property is acquired at the expense of a great many others. Marxism shares with anarchism the view that property is theft and that the pre-socialist state which protects personal property (specifically, the means of production) is *prima facie* a defender of injustice. Anarchists also believe that the concentration of power in a few hands over large territories and large aggregations of people destroys intellectual freedom.

It has already been mentioned that Sarvodaya principles are not based on the notion of the inalienable rights of individuals in the sense these rights have been articulated in Western liberal thought. These principles—*lokniti* (people's justice) based on *janasakhti* (people's power)—are a plea for genuine decentralization and devolution of political power as well as responsibility. There is considerable emphasis on *gramraj* (village government) on the grounds that a small-scale government can be responsive to individuals and cannot manipulate people as an amorphous aggregation, as masses. Sarvodaya's proponents agree with the anarchists and the Marxists that ultimately there must be only the management of things in a society and that such management must not lead to the manipulative use by some people of others.

Since we shall be discussing Bhave's more socialist views later, let us note that Gandhi's views about the state underwent some modification in the 1940s. He appeared to give up the notion of the abolition of the state as impractical and identified with Henry David Thoreau's proposition: that state is best which governs the least.

Gandhi is known more for his work for the attainment of independence than his propagation of Sarvodaya. Does not his nationalism, his passionate pleas for *Swadeshi*, imply that he was implicitly a supporter of the state? No. His opposition to British colonialism was based on the view that no one should be "the subjects" of another, whether foreign or domestic.

Excessive expressions of individualism, according to Bhave, lead to divisions, hostility, and egoism. He opposed representative democracy based on political parties and pleaded for a partyless democracy where the leaders would be nominated and elected by consensus using only two criteria: the record of their selfless service and the excellence of their character. The Sarvodaya emphasis on consensus formulation is very similar to that of Quakers (Society of Friends). The basic reason is the same: voting and majority rule often create more division than genuine progress.

The Sarvodaya ideology, especially as developed by Bhave, shares with Marxism the view that personalization of property is inimical to justice. Hence, the insistence that the rich must hold their wealth as trustees. Bhave gave the concept of trusteeship a stronger, socialist interpretation by proposing the eventual surrender of private property to collective will in small-scale socio-political units (Rolnick 1962).

The Marxist prescription for a dictatorship ruled by the proletariat as a necessary phase prior to the withering away of "the state" strikes Bhave as contradictory. Gandhi and Bhave assert that the patient propagation and practice of non-violent methods of conflict resolution must begin in the present. Said Bhave: "Assuming that we do not need government at all, we must begin today to work for its withering away" (Doctor 1964, p. 68).

Every able-bodied person doing at least some productive manual labor and every village (or similar small-scale community) producing and consuming enough for adequate food, shelter, clothing, and maintenance of essential services (for example, provision of water, roads, sewage disposal, etc.) would be two of the most effective ways to begin the task of dismantling the national state apparatus.

CONSCIENTIZATION AND MARXISM

Unlike Sarvodaya, the main articulators of Conscientization accept much of Marxist analysis. They do not accept the allegation that their work for liberation will culminate in their societies becoming like the state socialist dictatorships of the Soviet Union and eastern Europe where "dehumanized bureaucrats" rule the roost.

In Chapter 4 we noted that Conscientization was a term born in the context of economic and political struggles in a deeply Roman Catholic country, Brazil, and that the word became part of the vocabulary of Latin American liberation theologians. Therefore, like Sarvodaya, but unlike Marxism, Conscientization is founded in a belief in God. Adherents subscribe to the view that the complexity of human life cannot be reduced to historical materialism and that we must respect the transcendent dimension. There are many puzzling events in human life; it is dishonest to claim that the eventual development of a scientific socialism would help us to understand, let alone, solve all of them.

Yet, the proponents of Conscientization would agree with Marx:

Religious suffering is at the same time an *expression* of real suffering and also a protest against real suffering. Religion is the sigh of the oppressed creature, the sentiment of a heartless world, and the soul of soulless conditions* (Bottomore 1964, p. 43–44).

---

*The next sentence, of course, is: "It is the opium of the people."

In Conscientization, as in liberation theology, God takes the place of "the force of progress" in Marx. Conscientization is based on a socialist form of liberation theology. We shall use the two terms interchangeably in the following paragraphs.

Promoters of Conscientization do not accept Marxist teleology, namely the arrival of a classless society where the norm of "From each according to his ability; to each according to his need" would rule. As for Gandhi, so for Freire and others, the future is open for human construction. Yet, God's work which is the work of freeing human beings from the chains of oppression, must be done by human beings. Salvation is not only a matter of accepting Jesus as one's personal saviour, but also of carrying on the task proclaimed by Mary, mother of Jesus, in the Magnificat and begun by Jesus:

> He hath put down the mighty from their seats, and exalted them of low degree. He hath filled the hungry with good things and the rich he hath sent empty away.

There is thus a social, in addition to personal, dimension to salvation. Orthodox theologians often see sin as an ungodly personal thought or act; but, say liberation theologians, it is also a social thought or act. Christian churches emphasize personal sin but, perhaps out of fear or a desire for accommodation, do not point a finger at the perpetrators of social sins such as oppression. In a vein that would strike a responsive chord in many Hindus, Christians who support Conscientization emphasize the duty of human beings to work for salvation on earth in the present. They would accept Gandhi's view that there is enough on God's good earth to meet everyone's need but not to satisfy everyone's greed.

How does one work for salvation here and now? The adherents of Conscientization accept, in the main, Marxist class analysis to understand the present situation. There are oppressors in society and there are the oppressed. The oppressed will be able to recover or establish their humanity only when they struggle against the oppressors and the social systems which favor them. They assert that the oppressors also lose their humanity when they deal unjustly with the oppressed and that they too can become fully human only when exploitation and domination is eliminated. The social science basis of Conscientization is the "dependency" school of thought which claims that metropolises (such as the United States) keep hinterlands (like Brazil) in a relationship which enriches the former and improverishes the latter. The oppressed, say the proponents of Conscientization, have a duty to work toward the destruction of the present social system and establish a morally superior system.

Conscientization, then, differs from Sarvodaya in two respects. Sarvodaya as an ethical system does not advocate class struggle. It also makes no claim to the moral superiority of the poor as a group as against the rich in a society.

The proponents of Conscientization are somewhat inconsistent about the role of violence in bringing about social transformation. On the one hand, they emphasize the importance of democracy: participation, consultation, and regard for each other are hallmarks of democratic theory and practice. Yet, liberation theologians also recognize that violence may have to be at least condoned in certain situations. Christian theologians have, in the past, promulgated and defended the concept of "just wars." This tradition has given liberation theologians grounds for arguing for at least greater understanding for genuine wars of liberation.

The Sarvodaya hope that different classes can achieve reconciliation through a change of heart is, to Freire and others, self-deception. It is this stance, coupled with the necessity of struggle against the oppressors, that makes opponents of Conscientization see it as "Marxism-Leninism in Christian clothing." They, as King Henry II of England asked about Thomas Becket, would cry about a conscientized priest: Who will rid me of this troublesome priest?

Yet, guerrilla warfare would not be the first but the last step for adherents of Conscientization. For this reason, they are the objects of scorn among orthodox Marxist-Leninist revolutionaries. They denounce it as patronization, lack of courage, and wastage of effort in the attempt to awaken in a group of peasants the ability to analyze the causes and effects of poverty. The peasants or persons in similar situations know their context and difficulties. What is needed, say the orthodox Marxists, is for the peasants to take economic power since it is the source of other kinds of power (Koshy 1975, pp. 74-79).

Marxist-Leninist revolutionaries, more often than not, work under the discipline of a rigidly regulated Communist Party. They argue that party discipline is essential to be effective against the capitalist system's advantages and conspiracies. Liberation theologians and adherents of Conscientization tend to distrust communist organizations and prefer the apparently lesser efficacy of practicing democracy within their movements.

The proponents of Conscientization are similar to Gandhi and Bhave in their desire to create a responsive, caring community of persons. Yet, they do not state a preference for autonomous small-scale communities. They do not oppose the state as *inherently* evil. Neither do they denounce industrialization, as Gandhi did, as the source of inhuman exploitation. How may we explain this difference? The proponents of Conscientization understand social change in the same dialectical sense that Marxists do. To denounce industrialism is the exercise of naive idealism, as displayed, for example, by the Luddites in early nineteenth-century England. Technological inventions are human creations which can be used to reduce human misery. What matters is how it is done and to whose benefit. A detailed consideration of these questions is the task of Chapter 7.

The emphasis on education as a process of liberation is an extremely important facet of Conscientization, in contrast to Sarvodaya. We shall discuss in detail this difference in Chapter 6.

6

EDUCATION IN SARVODAYA AND CONSCIENTIZATION

> Conscientization...is a very strong Western concept. The Western tendency is to act upon reality, to confront reality and try to change it. The Indian tendency is to understand history as something in which you lose yourself....We have to take into account the cultural differences between East and West.
>
> Paulo Freire in Bangalore, India
> Quoted in Koshy 1975, p. 24

Education has an individual and a social dimension. It is a process, a means to an end, a symbol of status, and a social institution. We may think of education as it affects an individual in negative and positive ways: it is a process by which a person's ignorance is removed; it makes that person aware of the choices available to him or her to develop physically, mentally, and spiritually. Part of that awareness leads to an appreciation of the social nature of human life. A mother patiently teaching her child to speak a language is a social process and event; so is the dialogue between a teacher and a group of students. These social processes are a means to enable the new member of that society to participate in its culture. Within such a broad enabling goal are, of course, myriads of personal and group objectives: for example, to obtain a prestigious job; to display the credentials one has earned with hard work; to help raise the recognition of one's family in one's community, to ensure that members of one's family have access to the scarce positions and rewards of society; to achieve the satisfaction of helping others; to simply enjoy at least some products such as books or music or art in the treasure house of human civilization.

The examples of objectives listed above encompass both informal and formal education. Revitalization movements usually pay much attention to education, whether informal or formal, precisely because of its perceived ability to change attitudes, values, and behaviors in individuals. It is the task of this chapter to discuss the way proponents of Sarvodaya and Conscientization conceive of education and the role they attribute to it.

EDUCATION IN SARVODAYA

Sa vidya ya vimuktaye (education is that which liberates) is a well-known Sanskrit statement. That statement represents the quintessential Hindu view: human beings think or act in erroneous ways because of ignorance *(avidya)*; education *(vidya)* enables them to obtain higher and higher types of knowledge (for example, first, conceptual awareness of the empirical world; then, pure awareness about the eternal, absolute nature of Brahman—the eternal creator—and so on). Such knowledge leads a person to reject and be released (liberated) from the sufferings and attachments of the material world. This view formed the foundation (and hence was not obviously visible to everyone) of the Gandhian notion of education.

The more immediate Indian context was also influential in forming Gandhi's views. Ever since Thomas Babington Macaulay's Minute of 1835 the [British] government of India, with much support from the middle and upper middle classes, had created and extended a modern, Western type of formal education within India. Gandhi denounced this type of education as a profoundly alienating experience for Indians: the English language separated the modern urban Indian even more from his rural cousin than before the arrival of the Raj; the book-based, memory-taxing teaching which emphasized the acquisition of book knowledge prepared Indians only to become clerks and administrators in the offices of government, commercial houses, and so on. Gandhi said:

> I am convinced that the present system of primary education is not only wasteful, but is positively harmful. Most of the boys are lost to their parents and to the occupation to which they are born. They pick up evil habits, affect the urban ways and get a smattering of something which may be anything but education (Tendulkar 1962, vol. 4, p. 191).

Basic Education

Gandhi proposed, instead of such a harmful educational system, *nai talim*—literally "new education"—commonly known in

India as basic education. As we have already noted, Gandhi's vision of a new India was based on self-sufficient villages or groups of villages. The schools in these cooperative village democracies would create in the younger generation the desire and the ability to serve the community. Thus Gandhi's scheme of basic education had an organic tie with his vision of a new India.

How will basic education prevent problems of alienation and help develop a new society?

It will be free and compulsory for seven years. (The number was later changed to eight.)

The medium of instruction will be the mother tongue so that the English language as medium of instruction would not alienate the people from their own culture.

Gandhi was absolutely insistent on the use of the mother tongue as the language of instruction. Indians could not, he argued, creatively participate in the revitalization of their culture if they had to use an alien language. The imposition of the English language on Indians, Gandhi claimed, effectively cut them off from their roots and had warped their sense of personal identity. "The tyranny of English" had created far too much discontinuity between the home and the school. Although Gandhi was not an expert on the subject of the relationship of language to culture, his own experiences and observation led him to a stance with which many contemporary experts would agree.

Insistence on the mother tongue was only one of several proposals for the development of a new education. Education throughout the early years will center on some form of manual and productive work related to a handicraft such as spinning, cabinet making, etc. Thus every child will learn a productive skill which he or she can use in village life. In addition, all the children will learn to appreciate "the dignity of manual labor" which would eliminate one important ground for invidious caste and class distinctions.

Children will be spared the drudgery of learning any school subject for itself. The subjects will be related to the handicraft as well as the child's physical and social environment. This is known as the principle of *correlation*. For example, after a couple of hours of spinning, the teacher asks, say, five children the length of the thread each one has spun. Taking advantage of the different lengths each child reports, the teacher discusses the concept of average. On an earlier occasion he or she would have taught linear measurement to the class in a similar fashion. On an appropriate future occasion, he or she will discuss conditions under which cotton grows or relate the properties of circles to the spinning wheel. Extending the same principle, the child learns the rules of hygiene in the context of cleaning his or her classroom or school.* The principle of correlation rests on the psychological insight that active learning can be more interesting and relevant than passive learning.

By selling or bartering the products of children's manual labor basic schools can defray at least a portion of their costs. Gandhi wrote: "I have, therefore, made bold, even at the risk of losing all reputation for constructive ability, to suggest that education should be self-supporting" (Priest 1960, p. 156). A specific historical circumstance helped Gandhi take this extreme position. In 1937, in several British Indian provinces (excluding the princely states), congress ministries came into existence. They were committed to prohibition but were reluctant to lose the revenue from liquor taxes which would finance the expansion of formal education. Gandhi termed this "the cruellest irony of the new Reforms" and proposed self-supporting education as a way out (Nayyar 1952, p. 2). (This controversial idea was later dropped despite strong theoretical arguments that the self-supporting feature would hasten the universal provision of elementary education.)

Promotion and Decline of Basic Education

Although basic education was introduced on an experimental basis in the provinces in 1937, it was not actively promoted until after India's independence in 1947. From 1948 to 1956, a great deal of government energy at the federal level was expended to reform elementary education according to the principles of basic education. These efforts did not meet with success: compared to the rate at which new "three-R"-type schools were being established, very few new basic schools were opened; the conversion of traditional schools into basic schools fell far short of targets, and, observers noticed no significant differences between most basic and traditional schools in operation. The principles of basic education were also constantly challenged (*Report* 1959). Under these attacks, the proponents of basic education modified the principles to such an extent that by the early 1960s there was hardly anything left to differentiate between the principles of basic education and those of modern elementary education in advanced nations. N.V. Thirta's content analysis of, among other things, Government of India

---

*For these and other examples, see Ministry of Education, Government of India *Syllabus for Basic Schools* (Delhi: 1959), herein after referred to as *Report* 1959.

publications on basic education in the decade of the 1950s, ably documents this fact (Thirta 1959).

Gandhi and his educational disciples focused almost entirely on the education of children. (Only in the late forties did Gandhian educators propose new programs for adult education. In the thirties, the view appeared to be that adults would be too set in their ways.) This focus and the consequent neglect of the education of adults is understandable in the context of their wish to make a peaceful revolution. The assumption seemed to be that if children could be taught to have new values, attitudes, and skills, they would *eventually* change their society.

Gandhi's and Bhave's attempt to use formal education to help transform, in the first instance, India's villages was founded on a modern understanding of the role of education in society. The acquisition of knowledge can be related to two goals, one social, the other personal. The social goal is the transmission of a society's values, mores, and norms to assure its continuance. The personal goal, often mentioned by India's great philosophers, is the acquisition of knowledge to enhance one's efforts to attain spiritual salvation. It was in eighteenth-century Europe that, in the wake of the development of nationalism, formal education was used to indoctrinate children with the notion of loyalty to nation, ahead of loyalty to the church. Gandhi and his followers were indebted to Europe for discovering the possible transformative uses of formal education.

It has often been said that Gandhi proposed a regressive form of education. To some extent this criticism is valid. Yet, in fairness, we must note that the proponents of basic education hoped for three outcomes which were very progressive. The method of correlation was expected to show the "cause-effect" relationship of many natural occurrences to the children and thus eliminate superstition. The teachers were expected to work with children in a manner that would help them to develop a scientific attitude to the empirical world around them. Second, basic education was not against scholarly pursuits. Gandhi's criticism of bookish learning was not that learning from books was wrong. Indeed, he was an avid reader. He was against rote learning and memorization unaccompanied by understanding. Third, although Gandhi was clearly against the industrial civilization of the West, he was not against machines. He was opposed to the import and imposition of machines which enslaved people and sapped them of their creativity and responsibility.

Gandhian educators were vehemently opposed to the irrelevant and pointlessly abstract nature of primary education in India in the first half of the twentieth century. Yet, curiously, they prescribed the spinning wheel as the uniform remedy, as it were, to do away with the irrelevance of the existing curriculum in the approximately 600,000 different villages of India. Let us conclude this section with a quote from Vinoba Bhave:

> I am in the habit of going to see the work of any basic schools that happen to lie on the route of my Bhoodam pilgrimage. I ask the teachers where their own children are studying. The usual reply is that they are in Gaya or Patna or some such town. Why do they not keep their children with them, where father, and teacher, and a good type of education, are all to be had together? The reason, obviously, is that they have no faith in Nai Talim.
>
> Basic schools make khadi, but the children do not wear it. They are like hotels, where men prepare food for other people to eat.
>
> The wife of the village basic school teacher takes her children and goes and lives in the town. The children will undoubtedly learn one thing from her: "Son, whatever else you may do in the world, don't be such a fool as your father" (Bhave 1959, p. 202).

EDUCATION IN CONSCIENTIZATION

Perhaps a good way to begin this discussion would be to make the provocative point that for Freire, Gandhi's attempt to reconstruct society in part through the education of children would appear to be the manifestation of naivete. In "Education, Liberation and the Church," Freire says:

> Only the "innocent" could possibly think that the power elite would encourage a type of education which denounces them even more clearly that do all the contradictions of their power structures. Such naiveness also reveals a dangerous underestimation of the capacity and audacity of the elite. Truly liberating education can only be put into practice outside the ordinary system, and even then with great cautiousness, by those who overcome their naiveness and commit themselves to authentic liberation (1973a, p. 4).

Thus, whereas the focus of Sarvodaya has been mainly on the need for a new education for children, the focus of Conscientization is on adults, because of its wish to see changes occur in the foreseeable future. Also, we do not find in Conscientization any attempt to teach crafts, hygiene, etc. as we find in Sarvodaya. Such concrete measures must await the completion of the first revolutionary moment, the overthrow of the existing political-economic power system. Thus Freire played a part in helping the government of Guinea-

Bisseau—which came into being after the overthrow of Portuguese colonial rule following years of struggle—develop new curricular materials for elementary school children that do emphasize both Conscientization and practical arts and skills. Measures of alleviation, taken in an oppressive situation, merely provide some relief to the oppressing system, Freire would argue.

In Conscientization, in contrast to Sarvodaya, one finds a fairly sophisticated and elaborated discussion of andragogy, that is, principles and techniques for the effective teaching of Conscientization-based literacy to adults (see Table 6-1).

TABLE 6-1
STEPS IN CONSCIENTIZATION

---

1. Individuals in a "culture circle" WONDER AT the world instead of merely belonging to it and accepting *magical* explanations for events around them.
2. They DISTANCE or SEPARATE themselves as a first step to find their place in and with it.
3. They PROBLEMATIZE the world in terms of person-nature, person-person, person-culture, etc. categories.
4. They NAME their world; give literary expression to their place in time and space. They have reached the *naive* status of consciousness whose entire focus is on changing individual behavior.
5. They see their world in terms of the world of others and in terms of political, economic, cultural, etc. structures, that is, as a TOTALITY (TOTALIZATION). They reach the *critical* stage in which they can see the connection between individual and "system" behavior.
6. They begin—as individuals and in groups—to TRANSFORM *their* world.
7. Thereby they become SUBJECTS (not objects) and contribute to the HUMANIZATION OF the world.

Source: Compiled by author.

The abstract summary in Table 6-1, however, could be extremely misleading in that the process is not as orderly, predictable, or neat as shown here. It should be used only as a short-hand aid to comprehension.

Conscientization, then, is a theory promoting a specific kind of political education and action. It attempts to awaken or re-awaken in a person or a group the ability to analyze the causes and effects of an oppressive social system; the analysis must lead the person or the group to take responsibility for making changes in their lives and their society.

Oppression is prevalent in every part of the world but is widespread in the former colonies, which have become neocolonies and are often called the "Third World." Oppressive social systems promote "the banking concept of education" whereby knowledge is deposited in individuals to be taken out with interest later as the need arises. Such education denies to people their essential humanity, namely, the right and the responsibility to exercise their powers of reflective thought and freedom to choose.

Since Freire undertook his work in Brazil where the language of teaching-learning, Portuguese, is the same as the language of ordinary discourse, we do not find in his writings much discussion about the harmful effects of the imposition of a foreign language per se. In fact, the first time he had to face the problem of using another language was in Chile, where many of his Portuguese words and concepts were simply not appropriate or applicable. Yet, Freire is very much like Gandhi and Bhave in his outrage toward the imposition of alien forms of thought on people that clearly imply a severe devaluation of their own culture.

The process of Conscientization cannot begin without an avant-garde, a group of dedicated people who will spark interest and motivation in the oppressed people who have, in effect, resigned themselves to fatalism and magical explanations for their plight. This leadership group should not manipulate people for their own ends or transfer to them prepackaged knowledge. Freire's list of do's and don'ts for this group is quite formidable. Since many (or most) of the leaders would be from the middle class, they must be willing to commit "class-suicide." They must work with—not for—the poor. They should resist the temptation to be benign technocrats who impose solutions on the people; they should not arrogantly think of themselves as an all-knowing vanguard that does not consult the people they lead. In brief, they must be allies of the workers and peasants. They must preach and practice democracy and oppose "cultural invasion."

Freire is insistent that team leaders are not to be called teachers. They are expected to be "educator-educatees," animators, and the students "educatee-educators." These awkward terms are meant to convey the mutuality of the learning-teaching-learning process.*
Joel Spring rightly points out that Freire is anxious to avoid making objects out of students since that would contribute to more alienation in the sense Marx discussed it (Spring 1975, p. 69).

---

*In many Conscientization programs, illiterate adults are requested to teach some skill they know to the educator-educatees.

The literacy teams who worked with Freire in Brazil were apparently a group of such leaders.

The teams went to the world of the learners and listened to the language they used and the social and economic context in which that language was used. Freire had always emphasized the need to come into close, direct contact with the people of an area. From the language of the people, the team took words which met three criteria:

> they included the basic sounds of the language;
>
> when listed in sequence, the words enabled the adult student to move from simple letters and sounds to complex ones;
>
> the words were potentially useful in enabling the student to confront economic, political and cultural realities.

Freire did not use any primers or textbooks currently in use. He probably was involved in the development of the radical catechism *Viver e Lutar* (Live Through Struggle) of 1964. (See de Kadt's discussion of the contents of *Viver e Lutar* in *Catholic Radicals in Brazil,* pp. 156-62.) He probably used *Viver e Lutar* early in his work but did not continue using it.* The words chosen by the team were called "generative words" for two reasons: they could be broken down to syllables and used to form new words; they could generate discussion and dialogue about matters in daily life among the adult students. From experience, Freire discovered that in a syllabic language such as Portuguese, 16 to 20 words covered almost all the phonemes.

Since the words were taken from a specific locality, the list would be different in rural and urban areas. Many of the words Freire used in Brazil could not, after translation from Portuguese to Spanish, be used in Chile. He learned that the technique too must be changed to suit local conditions.

The literacy team used pictures and slides to introduce the words to the students. This process is known as "codification." The aim of codification is to initiate dialogue and action. The pictures appear on cards which (1) either depict words broken down into their syllabic parts or (2) show simple drawings which evoke dialogues about down-to-earth problems. These dialogues occur in a context ("the culture circle") different from that in which they live. The conversations assist the development of self-confidence of individuals who possessed little or none of it earlier. Perhaps, Freire's

---

*Collins claims that Freire's teams used *Viver e Lutar* (1977, p. 14). Other evidence does not completely support this assertion.

discussion of an occurrence in a culture circle in Sao Tome in the late 1970s would be helpful to understand codification:

> Among the numerous memories I have of the discussions in the cultural circles of Sao Tome, one that I found particularly moving was a visit to a circle in a small fishing community called Monte Mario. One of the generative words they were using was *bonito,* a common, local fish. The word was codified—illustrated—by a picture showing the village with its vegetation, typical houses, fishing boats in the sea, and a fisherman holding a bonito. The class first looked at the picture in silence, then four of them got up as if by arrangement and walked over to the wall where the picture code of the village was hung. They looked attentively at the picture, then they went over to the window and looked at the world outside. They exchanged glances, their eyes wide as if in surprise, and, again looking at the picture, they said, "It's Monte Mario. That's what Monte Mario is like, and we didn't know it." Through the picture code those four participants of the circle were able to put distance between themselves and their world, and to know it in a new way. In a certain sense it was as if they were "emerging" from their world, leaving it in order to know it better. That afternoon they had undergone an unprecedented experience: they had broken out of their narrow intimacy with Monte Mario and assumed a position as observing subjects, facing the small world of their daily routine (Freire 1981, p. 30).

Another example: a picture of a mud house can be used to show one's dependence on nature for the products used to make the house. A comparison of the mud house with that of a large brick house can lead to a dialogue of why some people are able to afford brick houses while others make do with mud ones.

Topical discussions like this are called "generative themes." The relationship between individuals in a "culture circle" is *intersubjective.* The dialogues would not only imprint the letters, words, and phrases in the student but enable him or her to recognize man's dependence on nature and how human beings create culture. In other words, the learner will recognize the distinction between the world of nature and the world of culture. Here the term "culture" is used in the anthropological sense and not in the sense of *Culto* which in Portuguese and Spanish conveys a meaning of polished literacy elegance. We must, says Freire, destroy the bourgeois notion of education as knowing a lot of alienating things. Freire calls his method scientific in its foundation and humanistic in its orientation.

Once the student learns that culture is what human beings create, the world becomes "problematized." Problematization is not problem-solving. "Problem-solving" is the technocrat's way of imposing solutions on people who have not participated in the decision. Problematization is an attitude based on curiosity, probing for relationships, and seeking knowledge to explain the relationships. The problematization enables the learner to "de-code" (demystify) one's own world, one's own experience. This decoding process enables the student to emerge from the "culture of silence" into a culture where he and she can name and speak "the word." The student, with others, can then construct a new code which should enable them to become subjects, to become members of human society, to create solutions to problems, to become makers—not passive witnesses—of history. They should now be able to become participants in *praxis,* whereby their practice informs their theory formulation and theory guides their practice.

To Freire, education is a value-laden activity. It is not neutral. Illiteracy, for instance, is not just a person's inability to read and write a language; it is part of an inability to "read reality"; it is part of an oppressive existence. It must not be reified. Certain individuals, groups, and social systems are responsible for this oppression and they must be identified and confronted. Freire believes in participation by the people in the economic, cultural, and political struggles of a society. This is what he means by democracy. If Freire has a Utopian vision, he is careful to insist that such a Utopia must be reached through historical struggles and, therefore, cannot be prescribed in detail ahead of time.

It is not hard to find defenders of liberal education in a middle or upper class university setting. Of course, the enlightenment one gets in the Kantian sense is mainly the result of private reflection. Freire, however, insisted that poor people in villages marked by muddy streets and in shanty towns made of corrugated iron, had as much right to a liberating education as the middle and upper classes. Freirean enlightenment arises from public, social practices (Matthews 1980, p. 87). See Table 6-2.

In *Education for Critical Consciousness,* Freire says that naive consciousness is

> characterized by an over-simplification of problems; by a nostalgia for the past; by underestimation of the common man; by a strong tendency to gregariousness; by a lack of interest in investigation, accompanied by an accentuated taste for fanciful explanations; by fragility of argument; by a strong emotional style; by the practice of polemics rather than dialogue; by magical explanations. (The magical aspect typical of intransitivity is partially present here also. Although men's horizons have expanded and they respond more openly to stimuli,

TABLE 6-2 BEFORE AND AFTER CONSCIENTIZATION

CLOSED SOCIETY	OPEN SOCIETY
Oppression is chief hallmark.	Liberation is chief hallmark.
"A Culture of Silence" is maintained, encouraged.	"A Culture of Dialogue" is made possible.
NAIVE CONSCIOUSNESS	*CRITICAL CONSCIOUSNESS*
Sustained by "banking" education.	Sustained by dialogic education.
Formal classroom.	"Culture circle": theoretic context to understand concrete events.
Teacher; student.	Animator/educator; educatee.
I know; you don't; I will teach you what is good for you; transfer systematized knowledge to you.	I know some things but so do you; I will work with you to learn our language; in the process you will also teach me many things. We will use your words as themes for discussions about your lives. "Problem-posing." They help us "de-code" reality as we experience it.
Authoritarian and hierarchical relationship between teacher and student. Teacher (active) student (passive)	E-E relationship is much less hierarchical; not authoritarian. Student and teacher are active.
Education is only subconsciously a political act; education for domestication.	Education is consciously a political act; education for liberation.
Promotes dependency.	Builds self-reliance, leads to cultural action for freedom.

Source: Compiled by author.

these responses still have a magical quality.) Naive transitivity is the consciousness of men who are still almost part of a mass, in whom the developing capacity for dialogue is still fragile and capable of distortion. If this consciousness does not progress to the stage of *critical transitivity,* it may be deflected by sectarian irrationality into fanaticism (Freire 1973b, p. 18).

Sarvodaya and Conscientization, with their revolutionary aspirations, emphasize moral development and give only secondary importance to intellectual growth and technical mastery as ends in themselves (see Wallace 1961).

Does Conscientization have naive expectations also? Has Conscientization been more effective, more successful than Sarvodaya in its educational mission? We shall examine that question in Chapter 8, keeping in mind the many dimensions and attributes of education noted at the beginning of this chapter.

7

ECONOMICS AND FUNDAMENTAL TECHNOLOGICAL CHANGE

> Our goal is not increased consumption but a vital standard; less in the preparatory means, more in the ends, less in the mechanical apparatus, more in the organic fulfillment. When we have such a norm, our success in life will not be judged by the size of the rubbish heaps we have produced; it will be judged by the immaterial and nonconsumable goods we have learned to enjoy, and by our biological fulfillment as lovers, mates, parents and our personal fulfillment as thinking, feeling, men and women. Distinction and individuality will reside in the personality, where it belongs, not in the size of the house we live in, in the expense of our trappings, or in the amount of labor we can arbitrarily command. Handsome bodies, fine minds, plain living, high thinking, keen perceptions, sensitive emotional responses, and a group life keyed to make these things possible and to enhance them—these are some of the objectives of a normalized standard.
>
> Lewis Mumford, *Technics and Civilization*

Revitalization movements are, as we noted in Chapter 1, sometimes spurred by what economists in the 1950s and 1960s called "the demonstration effect." Both Sarvodaya and Conscientization became movements because its proponents and their followers personally or surrogately witnessed, among other things, better material and social conditions in other societies and hoped to achieve improvements in their own societies. A consideration of the ideas implicit in Sarvodaya and Conscientization for improvement in the material standard of living of poor people necessarily leads us to discuss issues of political economy and technology.

Political economy, in a general sense, refers to the art and science with which corporate bodies (for example, families, governments) manage the resources of a people which includes the production and distribution of wealth. To produce wealth, human beings must work with the environment, by respecting or eliminating or modifying its constraints. Technology in its most general sense refers to the manner in which human beings modify "nature" in a systematic, practical way to produce artifacts which will, in turn, lead to the continuous development of culture. (Logically, material wealth and culture cannot be said to exist in a hypothetical society where human beings simply subsist. Yet, as Lewis Mumford warns us, tool-making and tool-using by themselves would not have created culture: "there was nothing uniquely human in tool-making until it was modified by linguistic symbols, esthetic designs and socially transmitted knowledge" [1967, p. 5]).

The political and economic dimensions of technological development figure in many discussions about the current crisis of human civilization. Do we need so many new products? Can we control the harmful effects of so many of them on us and our environment? How can we ensure that weapons of destruction are not made? Who should make decisions about technological advancement? Does capability to produce new things and techniques inevitably mean that they ought to be produced? These are some of the major questions that insistently arise. Problems of great magnitude in this area are with us because we are led to worship a quantitatively obsessed form of scientific endeavor, says Thomas Merton. Such worship makes people "one-eyed giants":

> The one-eyed giant had science without wisdom, and he broke in upon ancient civilizations which (like the medieval West) had wisdom without science: wisdom which transcends and unites, wisdom which dwells in body and soul together and which, more by means of myth, of rite, of contemplation, than by scientific experiment, opens the door to a life in which the individual is not lost in the cosmos and in society but found in them. Wisdom which made all life sacred and meaningful—even that which later ages came to call secular and profane (Merton 1965, p. 1).

Merton is surely exaggerating when he contrasts—in so extreme a fashion—wisdom with science. We may also point to the romanticism in his assertion that "pre-scientific" societies viewed all life to be sacred and meaningful. Yet, there is undoubtedly truth in his assertion: pre-modern communities were, to quote a recent author about a desirable type of society, "smaller, more controllable, more efficient, people-sized units, rooted in local circumstances and guided by local citizens" (Sale 1980, p. 37). Such communities retained the human scale not only in architecture, but in social arrangements, economic conditions, and political structures. Hence, people who are unhappy with societies dominated by monopoly capitalist institutions (for example, the United States of America) and socialist countries where the state reigns supreme (for example, the Union of Soviet Socialist Republics), search for a "Third Way" (Sik 1976).

Much of this chapter is about Sarvodaya's and Conscientization's attempt to contribute to the formulation of this third way. For reasons that will become evident later, much more attention is given to Sarvodaya than Conscientization.

TECHNICS AND HUMAN DEVELOPMENT IN SARVODAYA

Gandhi and Bhave—unlike Mounier, Camara, and Freire—had a Utopian vision for India. Utopians may be viewed positively as visionary reformers or pejoratively as impractical idealists proposing impossible schemes for perfecting human society. Let us, in this chapter, consider Gandhi, Bhave, and Freire as well as others as reformers with vision. We shall consider whether they were impractical dreamers in Chapter 8.

Gandhi's and Bhave's first premise was that the distinctive essence of Indian civilization is to be found in India's villages and that Indian cities were "a creation of foreign domination" (Gandhi 1952, p. 3). The revitalization of India's villages and the subordination of the cities to regional village councils were the main motivations that drove Gandhi. The following extensive quote portrays Gandhi's ideal village:

> My idea of village Swaraj is that it is a complete republic, independent of its neighbours for its own vital wants, and yet interdependent for many others in which dependence is a necessity. Thus every village's first concern will be to grow its own food crops and cotton for its cloth. It should have a reserve for its cattle, recreation and playground for adults and children. Then if there is more land available, it will grow *useful* money crops, thus excluding *ganja*, tobacco, opium and the like. The village will maintain a village theatre, school and public hall. It will have its own waterworks ensuring clean water supply. This can be done through controlled wells or tanks. Education will be compulsory up to the final basic course. As far as possible every activity will be conducted on the co-operative basis. There will be no castes such as we have today with their graded untouchability. Non-violence with its technique of Satyagraha and non-co-operation will

be the sanction of the village community. There will be a compulsory service of village guards who will be selected by rotation from the register maintained by the village. The government of the village will be conducted by the Panchayat of five persons annually elected by the adult villagers, male and female, possessing minimum prescribed qualifications. These will have all the authority and jurisdiction required. Since there will be no system of punishments in the accepted sense, this Panchayat will be the legislature, judiciary and executive combined to operate for its year of office. Any village can become such a republic today without much interference, even from the present Government whose sole effective connection with the villages is the exaction of the village revenue.... My purpose is to present an outline of village government. Here there is perfect democracy based upon individual freedom. The individual is the architect of his own government.

He and his village are able to defy the might of a world. For the law governing every villager is that he will suffer death in the defence of his and his village's honour.

The villagers should develop such a high degree of skill that articles prepared by them should command a ready market outside. When our villages are fully developed there will be no dearth in them of men with a high degree of skill and artistic talent. There will be village poets, village artists, village architects, linguists and research workers. In short there will be nothing in life worth having which will not be had in the villages. Today the villages are dung heaps. Tomorrow they will be like tiny gardens of Eden where dwell highly intelligent folk whom no one can deceive or exploit (Gandhi 1952, pp. 5-7).

Let us consider each of the following elements of Gandhi's and, later, Bhave's views: the importance of morality over materiality; the republican democratic nature of village government; self-sufficiency; informed, compassionate peasants as the architects of a new India, and, technology in the service of human needs.

Gandhi was firm in his view that the economy of a society must not be based on the continuous stimulation of demand for goods and services which then everyone scrambles to supply to themselves or to others. It was his view that if material wants can be kept to a minimum, people would have the time and the sense of tranquility to pursue nobler, non-material goals. E. F. Schumacher considered the modern Western view promoting economic growth fueled by greed to bring about development as

> standing the truth on its head by considering goods as more important than people and consumption as more important than creative activity ...shifting the emphasis from the worker to the product of work, that is, from the human to the sub-human (1968, p. 2).

Schumacher in this statement echoes Gandhi's view that spiritual and moral goals must guide economic policy instead of the pursuit of material wealth shaping and giving content to other personal and social goals.*

The proponents of Sarvodaya do not consider representative democracy (parliamentary, presidential, etc.) of the type now prevalent in Britain, India, France, and the United States as a desirable type of government. Representative democratic governments have become handmaiden to vested interests, they say. Their inevitable bureaucracies have alienated most of the people from governments. Only governments which are directly accessible to people can be both responsive and responsible. This is the source of the Sarvodaya view that villages of no more than a few thousand people should be the loci of governments. Such governments may form loose regional confederations. But such regional, state, or national governments must be subject to the control of the local governments. This view is obviously completely opposed to that of a strong central government deigning to devolve some of its decisions and functions to subgovernmental units for the sake of greater efficiency.

Most of Gandhi's writing is direct and prosaic. Yet, he is poetic in his defense of a definitely anarchistic vision:

> In this structure composed of innumerable villages, there will be ever widening, never ascending circles. Life will not be a pyramid with the apex sustained by the bottom. But it will be an oceanic circle whose centre will be the individual always ready to perish for the village, the latter ready to perish for the circle of villages, till at last the whole becomes one life composed of individuals, never aggressive in their arrogance but ever humble, sharing the majesty of the oceanic circle of which they are integral units.
>
> Therefore, the outermost circumference will not wield power to crush the inner circle but will give strength to all within and derive its own strength from it. I may be taunted with the retort that this is all Utopian and, therefore, not worth a single thought. If Euclid's point, though incapable of being drawn by human agency, has an imperishable value, my picture has its own for mankind to live. Let India live for this true picture, though never realizable in its completeness. We must have a proper picture of what we want, before we can have something approaching it. If there ever is to be a republic of every village in India, then I claim verity for my picture in which the last is equal to the first or, in other words, no one is to be the first and none the last (1952, p. 58).

---

*What was earlier known as the Gandhian view has become known more recently as the Buddhist approach to development (Sivaraksa 1980).

Why did Gandhi incorporate the notion of self-sufficiency in his manifesto for village republics? He understood—albeit insufficiently—the relationship between political freedom and economic independence. Hence, he insisted that each village must be basically self-sufficient in matters of food, clothing, and shelter. Such self-sufficiency in the kind of small-scale village republics Gandhi envisioned could not be a realistic goal unless everyone participated in physical labor. This was the practical reason for Gandhi's and Bhave's insistence on bread labor. Bhave even proposed that the currency of the villages should be based on some agreed upon units of physical labor (Sarva Seva Sangh 1973, pp. 65-66).

There were other reasons. If every able-bodied person in the village participates in physical labor, invidious distinctions based on caste and class would be seriously eroded. In Sarvodaya, the *charka* (spinning wheel) became a symbol for everyone making cloth for their own need and as a further symbol of the validity of bread labor. If everyone participates in labor that helps sustain people physically, they will have enough leisure to develop themselves mentally and spiritually. C. R. Yuille-Smith mentions the third reason: "The principle that a [person] must be remunerated... corresponding to his actual labour" is completely hostile to the doctrine of *karma* (1980, p. 663). One reaps as one sows in this and in one's succeeding births; differentiated wages reward one in this life itself which goes entirely against the way the universe works. It is this doctrine which led Gandhi to recommend bread labor and that everyone should view his or her additional profession—for example, as teachers, doctors, lawyers, government servants, etc.— to be as service to others which would help one attain perfection and thus escape the cycle of births and rebirths.

Even if one does not subscribe to a theory of reincarnation, the argument for donating one's labor, within limits, to the community makes sense. In a vibrant economy, many people donate part of their time and effort to ensure their community's survival and improvement. This provision of free labor produces a sense of ownership and pride in the community which, in turn, results in more economic activities that produce jobs. Gandhi and Bhave were keen to initiate a beneficial cycle of this nature in India's apathetic villages.

Gandhi considered the peasant as "the architect of a new order." Peasants lived close enough to the land to respect it and modify it when necessary with caution. They tended to live an unharried and leisurely life in a social milieu not marked by ruinous competition. These were, to Gandhi, virtues which could form the basis of a new social order if the peasants could be educated—through *nai talim*—to give up certain harmful attitudes and practices. We may note, in passing, Dandavate's opinion that in countries such as India, where the overwhelming majority of the population consisted of peasants, "there was no sense in evolving a Marxian model, considering the peasant as a conservative force and as a barrier in the path of industrialization and progress" (1977, p. 97).

Well-educated peasants would be in a good position to make discerning judgments about the kind of technology they would require to meet their needs. There is a widespread misconception that Gandhi and Bhave were opposed to machines as such. Oommen persuasively argues that such a misconception is uninformed propaganda. He quotes Gandhi: "...there would be no objection to villagers using even the most modern machines and tools they *can make* and *can afford* to use." Again, "I do visualize electricity, shipbuilding, iron works, machine-making and the like existing side by side with village handicrafts" (1981, pp. 591-92). Gandhi, thus, was not against industrialization. He was against urban industries destroying village industries and crafts. He reiterated the familiar theme that city industries must serve villages, not vice versa.

The Western idea of progress as a unilinear ever-ascending process in human society had no appeal to Gandhi and was rejected by the proponents of Sarvodaya. We must acknowledge that in the 1920s and 1930s, Gandhi anticipated the main lines of the debate about the "Quality of Life" crisis in the West in the 1970s. E. F. Schumacher helped popularize the concept of the human scale in his by now classic work *Small is Beautiful* (1973).

TECHNOLOGY AND CONSCIENTIZATION

The literature on Conscientization does not contain much, if any, discussion about the technological and political nature of the new social order that would replace capitalist society. One possible explanation may well be the source of the concept and the movement, namely, Brazil. Unlike India where the nature of the village life helped to define the nature of her civilization, contemporary Brazil is, literally, the imposition of a European imperial nation on cultures and peoples who were eventually destroyed or absorbed. There is thus in Brazil nothing like "a golden age" that its people can use to dream the vision of a bright future. Another explanation might be traced to Conscientization's acceptance of Marxian analysis. Technological developments in capitalist society are seen, principally, as the result of the bourgeoisie's attempt to reduce labor costs. The nature of technological developments in a genuinely socialist society will be the result of new forces and relations of production which cannot be anticipated now because we can only see the outlines of that new society "as through a glass, darkly." Therefore, there is in Conscientization a focus on immediate objectives and intermediate goals.

Yet, Conscientization's critique of capitalism is similar in many respects to Sarvodaya's critique of mass industrialization. Conscientization's use of Marx's concept of alienation—the process by which capitalism objectified the worker into an abstract thing called labor—finds a clear echo in the Sarvodaya literature. Both approaches agree that technology is not neutral and it must help improve and enhance people's lives. The Marxist critique of the increasing miserliness of the proletariat finds a parallel in Gandhi's and Bhave's denunciation of the continuous pauperism of India's villages. The masses are exploited, manipulated, and deprived of their dignity, says Marx. Gandhi and Bhave would agree. There must be new political institutions in which ordinary men and women can participate and contribute to policy formation and implementation, say the Marxists. There, too, the Gandhians agree. The ideal future society will be both classless and stateless say Marxists and Gandhians in a chorus.

The differences between Gandhians and advocates of Conscientization are significant too.

Gandhians believe that all forms of life have souls and that a rabbit, a cow, or a plant we see today may well have been a human being in an earlier incarnation. Many of these so-called lower creatures live very close to nature; any attempt to change vast landscapes or kill any animals for the benefit of people will affect the entire balance of nature. Technological improvements must be respectful of the lower orders of the animal and plant kingdoms. Conscientization, rooted in part in the Biblical view that God has given Man dominion over other beings and nature, has a far more instrumental view of the role of technology.

In Gandhi's and Bhave's writings, one finds a clear rejection of massive industrialism. Gandhi associated the development of mammoth industries of the type that produced prosperity in the West as profoundly alienating and dehumanizing. He and Bhave sincerely believed that only small communities which produced most of all the things and services for their needs could be attentive to the needs and concerns of every individual. Camara, Freire, and other proponents of Conscientization do not address the question of whether industrialization in itself is an evil. Their view is that alienation and dehumanization are the consequences of the undemocratic manner in which industries are managed. There is nothing inherently evil in industrialization per se.

In fact, advocates of Conscientization go further. They reject as hopelessly naive and romantic the Gandhian call to ordinary people to live a simple life not cluttered up by the possession and entanglements of too many material goods. While being critical of the way in which the benefits of technology have been distributed to people, they point to the many modern inventions that have made life more bearable for everyone. Pre-industrial feudal society, they would point out, had as many attractive as ugly features; we must not ignore those ugly aspects. For example, in pre-industrial Europe, most people lived brutal, squalid, disease-ridden, hungry lives which were, for the most part, mercifully short. Provisions for far greater participation for, and consultation among, the people will ensure that technological progress will serve human ends, proclaim the promoters of Conscientization. It is the unbridled search for profits that makes technology anti-human, not some intrinsic property in technological logic. They would agree with Ota Sik:

> Just as bureaucratic state ownership offers no remedy for alienation from the means of production, so responding to capitalist, or communist, alienation of human labour by crusading against economic efficiency—essentially a petty-bourgeois reaction—affords no solution for our problems. No resistance to technological progress, no renunciation of material consumption, no back-to-nature ideas can banish the conflicts now bedevilling social production. Radical groups wedded to these ideas are fated to remain sects, as incapable as religious sects of persuading the majority to change their ways. The present perversion of consumption, imposed by the weight of one-track interests, can be cured solely by democratic means, finding new channels through which the public can share, in growing measure, in economic and political decision-making (1976, p. 410).

Another significant difference is in the perception of the place of urban areas in society. The Sarvodaya view is clearly that urban centers dominate, exploit, and weaken the rural areas which produce the real wealth of a society. There is no discussion about this question in the literature on Conscientization. A reasonable inference, however, would be that its view of cities is far more benign than that of Sarvodaya: cities do dominate the hinterland but they also provide opportunities for personal and social development. The next chapter will deal with critiques of the two approaches.

8

PROPOSALS FOR IMPLEMENTATION: CRITIQUES AND OPPOSITION

James Cameron, a British journalist, tells a story of how Gandhi came to New Delhi in 1946 to talk to members of the visiting British Cabinet Mission. He had decided to live in a hut in an area where "untouchables" had traditionally lived. He would thus show his oneness with them. Of course, to make the hut habitable for the Mahatma, electric lights, telephones, bathrooms, and fans were quickly installed. Approach roads were repaired and the entire area was cleaned up.

> Ah, said Mrs. [Sarojini] Naidu [Gandhi's friend and collaborator], surveying this elegant scene, the only Untouchable Quarter in India with all modern conveniences, "if the Mahatma only knew what it costs *us* for him to live the simple life" (Cameron 1974, p. 93).

This anecdote exemplifies many of the dilemmas we shall explore in this chapter. Sarvodaya and Conscientization are, in the first instance, protest movements. But they provide to their followers a vision about the kind of humane social order they must work toward. Is this vision a Utopian one in the worst sense of the word, that is, an ersatz, syncretic hodgepodge? Our analysis will not focus on strictly conceptual critiques based on human nature, nature, technology, and so on. The emphasis, instead, will be on critiques based on practical considerations which, of course, have underlying theoretical predispositions.

SARVODAYA'S APPROACH TO SOCIAL RECONSTRUCTION

There is now a widely prevalent view which presumes that desire for continuous material improvement is natural to human beings. The origins of this view may be traced to the development of capitalism in Western Europe. The Gandhian approach to personal development and societal reconstruction, based on modern reinterpretations of ancient Hindu scriptures and social organization, rejects this view. Any fair critique of the Sarvodaya approach to social reconstruction must acknowledge—which is not to say, accept—this fundamental premise. The Sarvodaya approach emphasizes that basic human needs—food, clothing, shelter, health care, and a sense of security in a community—must be provided to everyone; thereafter, the organization of society must actively discourage the pursuit of material abundance which will foment greed, a definite evil disposition. People must be encouraged to pursue their personal goals, in a non-attached way, to serve society, thereby forming their unique identities.

The Relationship of Materiality and Morality

Material conditions do not exclusively determine our mores any more than our moral notions exclusively determine the way we relate to others or to the material world. There is an undeniable dialectical relationship between the material world and the ideas with which we deal with that world. Controversies about extreme forms of materialism and idealism are worse than useless. The nature and extent of human agency, on the other hand, can provide us with more useful points of departure.

The Sarvodaya approach proscribes selfishness and prescribes selfless service. Such a view ignores the diverse well-springs as well as consequences of human motivation. Human beings desire and therefore attempt to provide for their own and their family's material needs and sense of self-worth. In this process, they will act in ways that are at times selfish and at times generous. Sometimes their ostensibly selfish acts are inadvertently helpful to others just as at other times their ostensibly humanitarian acts will inadvertently diminish others. It is also commonplace to note that many professed generous acts have hidden selfish motives. The manner in which one's motives are shaped depends only in part—nevertheless significantly—on the way one relates to the natural world as well as to other people to meet one's basic needs. In this process of relating to other human beings, simple curiosity as well as desires for prestige, recognition, capacity to influence others, the acquisition of more material goods, etc. play their part. The Sarvodaya claim that these complex patterns of motivation are all, in effect, the result of ignorance, avoids too many issues.

This is not only a philosophical argument. Ram refers to the people of the village of Baranpur (of the Meja Tehsil, Allahabad district) who offered their village in *Gramdan* (1962, pp. 479-81). A gentleman interviewed several people about this decision. The following conversation between him and a widow with a seven-year-old son (her only child), who donated 30 acres, conveys the tenor of the sentiments expressed.

> "You have given all your land. But in case your eyes are closed tomorrow, who shall look after your child?"
>
> With a determined calm on her face, she remarked, "Now that the whole village has turned into one family, all my worries have disappeared. The village family will play such a good guardian to my son that no father or mother can." And she added: "I will die a very happy death" (Ram 1962, p. 480).

Far be it for us to devalue the report of this woman's noble action and great faith. There are indeed noble individuals and ordinary people who make noble and heroic gestures. However, we may note that during the height of the cultural revolution in China (1966-69), magazines such as *China Reconstructs* and *China Pictorial* carried several articles with similar statements. In the post-cultural revolution period, beginning in 1976, these assertions have appeared ludicrous because they falsely gave the impression that *large numbers of human beings* had become selfless servants of socialist ideals.

We need not merely refer to China to raise questions about such claims. Sachchidananda et al.'s excellent empirical study (1976) of the efficacy of Sarvodaya in the Musahari Block in the district of Muzzaffarpur, Bihar, was described in some detail in Chapter 5. The unmistakable conclusions of the study are two. Gross and crude exploitation had decreased; gambling and alcoholism had decreased, and, a large number of landless laborers had received title to their homesteads and could no longer be evicted. But, these improvements only provided some relief to the existing politico-economic system.

> There was some evidence to suggest that the *Sarvodaya* movement strengthened rather than weakened the semi-feudal bondage....[According to one of the authors,] the rural rich have continued to grow economically and politically by cornering the bulk of the benefits flowing out of the development work...under the auspices of Sarvodaya (Sachchidananda et al. 1976, p. 109).

These conclusions confirm that although the concept of class has ambiguities that irritate some logicians, politicians, etc., class is real enough in the lives of people. Class considerations drive people in India and elsewhere to act to increase their political and economic power or at least to prevent further losses of such power.

The Role of Persuasion and Education

Gandhi's and Bhave's view that *nai talim* (basic education) would help form the character of children in a manner that would support the Sarvodaya approach to society is an important extension of the hope that persuasion can be effective in changing attitudes and values. Persuasion can be accomplished in two principal ways: verbal communication in schools and in other educative contexts, and more important, living according to the principles one professes.

Obviously, persuasion has not been successful in making Sarvodaya a reality in Indian society. It is, of course, possible to change "human nature." Sometimes, such changes can be brought about in individuals through persuasion. But if large aggregates of individuals, that is, groups (which are more than the sum of their parts) are to change, both material conditions and moral expectations have to change hand in hand. Thus we are compelled to disagree with Gandhi's and Bhave's view that true civilization is manifested only in societies that promote the reduction of wants. Excessive personal addiction to or greedy pursuit of material goods is not evidence of civilization. Nor is life civilized for one who rigorously eschews most technological advances and material comforts on grounds of principle.

We may illustrate this mediated conclusion with the concept of bread labor. Every major proponent of it has been a middle or upper class person (Bondaryev, Tolstoy, Ruskin, and Gandhi) to whom some manual labor may well have provided welcome relief from non-manual preoccupations. We have noted in Chapter 6 that the valuable insight in the concept is that the widespread implementation of "bread labor" would reduce the dependence of small-scale communities on external political, economic, and cultural forces. In Gandhi's ideal village, most economic activity would necessarily have to be based on barter or a modified form of barter. However, as Sohn-Rethel (1978) has pointed out, the concept of money is an important intellectual abstraction that has facilitated the formulation of other abstractions leading to technical development and material progress. Gandhi and Bhave were very aware of the harmful (sometimes unintended) consequences of technical progress but seemed to have little appreciation for the beneficial consequences of socio-economic development.

In Sarvodaya, the possibility exists that one can apprehend and attain truth by a series of personal, self-purifying actions. In Conscientization, truth has a strong social dimension; it arises out of concrete experiences in a particular time and place. This emphasis leads Conscientization to an acute awareness of the political nature of many philosophies and the development of techniques to learn new truths that serve to liberate oppressed people. In Sarvodaya, for example, the learning of crafts such as spinning and weaving by children has little or no political content. They may learn, for instance, about how cotton is grown and how its spinning and weaving will lead to the creation of clothes. But there is no attention given, for instance, to the way the big cloth-mill owners in Bombay pay very little to the cotton growers of the hinterland or how they do not share their profits with workers. Discussion of such matters is essential in Conscientization.

Gandhi and Bhave exhorted professionals (medical doctors, lawyers, teachers, etc.) also to participate in bread labor. When not engaged in it, they were to provide their services to people without any thought of monetary remuneration. This exhortation, again, ignores the complexities of human motivation. In India, as in many other countries, people enter the professions not primarily to serve humanity but to acquire the symbols of prestige, many of which are material goods and services. Manual laborers themselves do not, to the best of our knowledge, seek a balance between manual and mental labor. They accept the necessity of manual labor to meet their basic needs. If they have a choice, they would prefer *rising to* occupations demanding mental work in place of manual labor. Any attempt to find a balance, they know "instinctively," will favor those who are currently involved in predominantly mental labor occupations. That is the primary reason for the failure of attempts to ruralize the curriculum of schools in India, China, and several other countries. A "ruralized school" appears as an absurdity to peasants: Why should their children go to school to learn things that the peasant-parents can teach better? Indeed, the latent function of a ruralized curriculum is clearly manifest to the peasant parents: as the country cousin of the better urban school, the rural school will keep peasant children in the village and at the bottom of the socio-economic ladder.

Resistance to school reforms of this type used to be attributed to the stupidity, inertia, traditionalism, and so on of peasants, workers, or whoever happened to oppose plans and programs developed in urban (central or other) government offices. We now know, thanks to the work of Marriott (1952), Harris (1974), and Bhattacharya (1966)—to mention only three among a host of scholars—that the interrelationships between technics and cultural practices are such that new technical changes or proposals for changes in cultural practices will require several readjustments to minimize the disruptive effects of the new addition. Conservatives have used the interrelationship thesis to argue, in effect, for maintenance of the status quo ante. My point is distinctly different: proposals for the introduction of new techniques or new cultural practices are inevitable in today's world. But their introduction should use criteria that will advance—not retard—the welfare of the people affected. One of the most effective ways of doing so is to work with the people affected as much as possible and not impose solutions on them.

Formal education for millions of children from all social classes is no more than a century old in many parts of the world. Ever since the expansion of formal educational systems made access for adults (other than kith and kin) to children and youth more possible, social reformers have consistently looked to the school to help build a new social order. For a whole set of reasons, schools cannot be the prime movers to bring about significant social change.

What are these reasons? Most adults see schools as institutions charged with the responsibility of *transmitting* to the young values that are apparently widely accepted in society; they do not accept the view that schools ought to work for the short-run transformation of those values. The persons who control the dominant economic and political institutions in society perceive the school as an institution performing socialization tasks set for it by them; they will suppress any attempt by educational leaders who chose to undertake re-socialization activities which will threaten the position of dominant economic and political elites. Other than in exceptional cases, the majority population in schools which consists of young people cannot be realistically expected to lead a movement to change adults and their ways of life. Even if all the adults in schools—mainly teachers and school administrators—were sincerely committed to social reform, they are too few and usually are too low in the prestige scale of occupations to significantly influence adult society. Of course, most adults in school are often ill-prepared to introduce changes in school curriculum to usher in social changes (Zachariah and Hoffman 1985). Moreover, there are usually too many other demands on the time and energy of teachers. This is another way of pointing out that those who would use the school as an agent of social reform are either unwilling or unable to provide it with the material resources to promote the reform.

Villages and Peasants as Locales and Sources of Good Government

Adi H. Doctor evaluated the possibility of a non-state society and found it exceedingly wanting on philosophical, logical, and practical grounds (1964, chap. 6). It is not necessary to repeat here the arguments he advances other than to summarize the relevant ones.

The Sarvodaya view that human beings are inherently good is a statement of faith and not a conclusion based on evaluation of evidence. The anarchist position that cooperation rather than competition characterizes society is a depiction of harmony *within* castes or tribes and not about harmony *between* them. The view that society can be like a family ignores crucial differences between the two entities. There is no logically sustainable relationship between the enjoyment of material comforts and turpitude. Indeed, material development may well be a *sine qua non* for moral development. Gandhi's success in using non-violent methods to end British rule in India does not mean that he converted the hearts and minds of those in authority. The British decided to transfer power to Indians because their position as rulers had become untenable. It is far too simplistic to consider the state as an inherently evil institution. The state can bring about income redistribution to elevate the living standards of desperately poor people which is far more practical than expecting rich people to make *sampattidan* (gifts of their wealth) because they have seen the error of their ways. The Sarvodaya view does not address the practical details of how a non-state society operating on a partyless, consensus basis will avoid the evils of statism. Indeed, the likelihood is that such a society could be far more oppressive than an oppressive state. Concepts such as *prajasakthi* (people's power) in Sarvodaya are too nebulous and ignore class, caste, religious, regional, and family antagonisms that constitute the fabric of village life. Ideally, small-scale societies may be more caring entities but the cost tends to be the sacrifice of privacy and a sense of personal space to pursue one's interests, as many inhabitants of small towns who flee to the anonymity of urban life readily testify.

The Sarvodaya approach believes that peasants can be a source of change. Peasants, like any other group, can be agents of significant social change as Mao Ze-dong so conclusively demonstrated in the 1930s and 1940s in China. But mystical faith in them or in the proletariat to bring about a humane social order is unrealistic. It is necessary to pay attention to what radical politicians call ideological consolidation, that is, showing to those elites who control economic and political decisions that a *numerically* superior group which cannot easily be divided and ruled is prepared to be an effective counterveiling political force and, therefore, must be dealt with seriously.

During the decade of struggle for Indian independence, Gandhi and his Congress followers were able to be a powerful counterveiling force to the British colonial government. But, in independent India, the Sarvodaya leaders neglected political activity, indeed declared non-participation in party politics to be their distinguishing virtue. Oommen is right to castigate this Sarvodaya attempt to be "pure" at the cost of attaining important goals (1979; 1981).

The Sarvodaya leaders may retort that the kind of political movement they would like to spearhead is the kind that resulted in Indian independence, that is, one in which people from many classes, castes, religions, and regions came together to overthrow colonialism. That argument, while valid within limits, has two serious problems. First, within the independence movement there were extremely serious differences of opinion which were glossed over until the attainment of independence; they began to surface immediately thereafter. From that point onwards, it was the national bourgeoisie who controlled the direction of the economy even when the Congress party was paying lip service to the creation of a "socialistic pattern of society" (a nice, vague phrase). Multiclass movements can be effective in the short term, for example, to overthrow an insufferable tyrant or to end colonial rule but they are not effective agents for long-term change. If in India, the national bourgeoisie coopted the independence movement, in Nicaragua the Sandinista government has so far managed to avoid that outcome, as it continues its struggle not to be overthrown covertly or overtly by the U.S. government.

Das Gupta chides the Sarvodaya movement for preaching "trusteeship" to the rich and the powerful instead of focusing on

Gandhian civil disobedience by the oppressed (1969, pp. 31-35). The choice of the Sarvodaya leadership is, politically, a realistic one. A series of civil disobedience campaigns would put the Sarvodaya movement in direct confrontation with the Indian state. The state would then be moved to suppress the movement or to make genuine concessions. The record suggests that it would do the former, not the latter. The two major consequences would be that the Sarvodaya movement would not be able to maintain its non-violent stance and the state would be compelled to drop its liberal democratic stance, as we shall show later.

Critics and even sympathizers of the non-violent approach to social change have noted that its proponents tend to be middle-class individuals who take a "hard" personal radical stance on particular matters without directly confronting the root causes of the problem (Miller 1960). They thus feel that they are doing something important and are on the side of justice without too much personal cost. Such liberal stances do not bring about significant social change, at least not in the short run.

Sarvodaya as a movement requires a government that is democratic in the sense in which Canada and India are democracies where election by secret ballot exists and constitutional guarantees regarding freedom of speech, freedom of assembly, protection against unlawful arrest, and so on have a reasonable possibility of enforcement in relatively independent courts of law. It has been said that Gandhi first learned of the efficacy of Satyagraha from his wife who would silently suffer his indiscretions and excesses in a manner that would unmistakably get the message to him. Gandhi changed his behavior when faced with his wife's non-violent non-cooperation because he loved and respected her. In the arena of political change, Satyagraha tactics require similar mutuality of respect. One of the remarkable facets of the Indian movement for independence was the high regard Gandhi had for many aspects of the British way of life and the respect with which many British colonial administrators treated him. The world of the 1980s is very different from that of the 1930s and 1940s. Even in liberal democratic societies, physical elimination of political enemies seems to be a more common occurrence now than was the case then. Thus Sarvodaya is in a dilemma. It can choose to respect the limits of its principles and those of political democracy thereby condemning itself to inefficacy. Or it can choose to achieve its goals by compromising its principles and exploiting the weaknesses of political democratic governments. If it chooses the latter course of action, of course, the government would not remain idle and passive.

Without in any manner denigrating the freedoms and protections enjoyed by citizens in political democracies, we must note that, as states, they are required to protect and defend personal and corporate property. Sarvodaya—a socio-political movement which preaches the necessity for revolutionary change in matters which include property relations, while proclaiming non-violence and voluntary giving of gifts—does not ever need force the state to bare its, as it were, iron hand hidden in the velvet glove. The price Sarvodaya pays, of course, is enormous: credibility and efficacy.

No significant social change for good or ill can come about without violence, without violating earlier political, economic arrangements or social mores. Gandhi would agree with this claim and would have proposed mass Satyagraha as an active way to promote the necessary *psychological* violence of making the opponent feel guilt, shame, etc. Post-Gandhian Sarvodaya leaders, as we have seen, chose not to exercise that option.

Gandhi's condemnation of industrialism has often been criticized for mistakenly attributing to industrialism evils which should accurately be attributed to the capitalist form of industrialism. We have not yet seen much evidence of how a socialist form of industrialism would be significantly different from the capitalist form to increase the personal autonomy of people. China's abandonment of the principles of the cultural revolution raises anew the profoundly disturbing issue of whether certain forms of organizing and motivating human beings is intrinsic to "human nature" as we can apprehend it now, rather than to forms of economic organization and consequent political as well as cultural institutions.

CONSCIENTIZATION AND REVOLUTIONARY CHANGE

As in the case of Sarvodaya, Conscientization also requires a liberal democratic government to become a movement for change. Since we have discussed the limits and possibilities that Sarvodaya faces, there is no need to repeat them for Conscientization, except for a brief discussion of the role of education. It, like Sarvodaya, faces a hard choice between efficacy and wide acceptability.

Conscientization's proposals for focusing on oppressed adults and working with them to develop their political awareness and sense of self-worth appears, in the first instance, to be more practical than Sarvodaya's prescription for *nai talim* involving mainly children and youth. Yet, Conscientization too faces the same challenge as does Sarvodaya: when the elites see it as a developing threat, they will move to smother it. Brazil and Chile are witness to that factual conclusion. Or, Conscientization becomes coopted into the existing system and thus is unable to bring about any major structural changes in society (Kidd and Kumar 1981; Ewert 1981).

Unlike Sarvodaya, Conscientization may be criticized for not proposing concrete measures for improving the standard of living of the people. It is—far more than Sarvodaya—an educational program in the widest sense of the term. We have already noted two other reasons for this neglect. The economic program for reconstructing society, according to Conscientization, must await the people taking power, albeit through "acceptable" means. Since Conscientization has a far more benevolent and dialectical understanding of the role of technology in society, its proponents did not feel compelled to offer a new—basically pre-industrial—vision of the good society.

Conscientization may also be criticized, as we have already noted, for being patronizing in its own way. Do ordinary men and women need to be conscientized before they recognize that they lead desperate, oppressed lives marked by hunger, disease, and the denial of dignity? They know the score and do not need middle class do-gooders to tell them. They acquiesce in their oppression because they have no other choice, say the critics. To offer them hope through Conscientization is worse than deceitful. What they need is for people to fight on their sides, so that they can overthrow the oppressors.

Conscientization has been criticized for evading, or worse, camouflaging the issue of leadership. No amount of talk about "educator-educatees" and "educatee-educators" can get around the fact that there are teachers and students in Conscientization, say the critics. It is a short step from that criticism to characterize the leaders of culture circles—not benevolently as "teachers"—but as meddlesome, outside agitators.

Conscientization may also be criticized for not promoting the vision of a different economic order such as "the replacement of demand-oriented production by need-oriented production" that Sarvodaya propounds (Sethi 1977, p. 134).

Can Conscientization be fully respectful of other cultures? Freire is strongly opposed to attempts to impose one's culture on another. Critics, however, have pointed out that the team leader could not help leave his or her imprint on the team. An even more fundamental criticism has been brought up by Bowers (1983). He identifies several elements in Freire's pedagogy that is exclusively Western:

the view that people are or can be agents of historical change; belief in the possibility of progress; the conviction about the power of critical reflection; the emphasis on the uniqueness of human beings; the importance of respecting individuality; faith in socialism; and so on. The earlier chapters have documented the differences between (Western) Conscientization and (non-Western) Sarvodaya. Bowers, however, raises the question of whether a pedagogy which opposes cultural invasion can, unwittingly, be hegemonic and promote a new kind of cultural imperialism in non-Western areas of the world.

A final criticism of Conscientization is that it does not confront the fact that there are no local solutions to many of the problems of which the conscientized adults become aware. We may recall that, unlike Sarvodaya, Conscientization does not propose more or less self-sufficient small-scale societies to replace nation-states. Given that position, Conscientization appears not to have solutions to problems of peasants in, for instance, the interior of northeastern Brazil created in the board rooms of New York and Toronto.

In Chapter 9, we shall discuss the technical and other possibilities and problems of comparing Sarvodaya and Conscientization.

9

COMPARING REVITALIZATION MOVEMENTS: DIMENSIONS, BENEFITS, PITFALLS

> If a man does not keep pace with his companions, perhaps it is because he hears a different drummer. Let him step to the music which he hears, however measured or far away.
>
> Henry David Thoreau, *Walden*

We compare people, ideas, events, and things implicitly or explicitly much more often than we recognize. Often, we do not notice the pervasive presence of comparison in scholarly endeavors. Many descriptions and analyses of an unfamiliar event in another culture, for example, are unavoidably based on the scholar's real or assumed familiarity with roughly similar events in his or her own culture. Many apparently universal propositions about human nature and society are based on such implicit comparison or, put another way, comparison by implication. Many such propositions would not stand the test of a more conscious, formal comparative investigation.

More consciously formulated comparative investigations are undertaken in every major discipline of the natural sciences, social sciences, humanities, and professional studies. They are undertaken often because at least some scholars say that one can understand, for example, an institution or a process well only if we study it comparatively. The focus of this chapter is on explicit attempts to undertake comparative study.

Gopala Sarana considers comparisons to be of three types: illustrative comparison (casual), complete universe comparison (delineated), and, holegeistic comparison (sampled-statistical) and discusses the technique, purposes, areal coverage and units and categories of each (1975, p. 70).

In the humanities, social sciences, and professional studies, our interest in pursuing comparative studies may be kindled for a number of reasons.

Donald Johnson referred to seven reasons that impel people to study people, nations, and cultures other than their own, although he referred to them as seven "levels of consciousness":

1. as a setting for the history of one's nation or civilization;
2. as a problem for the foreign policy of one's country;
3. as part of the campaign against stereotyping in one's country;
4. as part of the attempt to learn about the uniqueness of each culture [including one's own] as it has developed over time;
5. as part of the effort to create empathy for all human beings;
6. as a case that exemplifies comparative social science research and application; and
7. as an attempt to understand a unique culture's particular answers to humankind's universal questions (Fersh 1978, pp. 24-26).

In the case of this study, objectives 4, 5, 6, and 7 are the relevant ones.

Among significant groups of social scientists, comparative studies are undertaken in the hope that they will lead to the apprehension of underlying principles which govern all societal systems despite apparent differences, to tease out "forces and factors" that produce the similarities as well as the differences, and, to speculate with greater confidence about future trends from what we know about the past and the present.

Professional disciplines and fields acknowledge the humanist's search for deeper understanding and the social scientist's hope for control and prediction. Their focus in pursuing comparative study is on providing the basis for advocating change either within one's own culture by selective borrowing or in another culture by selective transplantation. In some instances, change both within and without may be deemed simultaneously desirable. Professional studies do promote the development of humane sensitivity to the circumstances of other persons, cultures, and nations, although such emphasis is not exclusive to professional studies.*

---

*Within educational studies, a distinction between comparative education (as scholarly, objective analysis) and international education (as the active promotion of international contacts and knowledge) has been asserted (Fraser and Brickman 1968, p. 1). For reasons that are advanced later in this chapter, I consider the distinction untenable.

There are two extreme positions that some scholars take which deny the possibility and the utility of comparing cultures. The first objection questions the usefulness of comparative study. It claims that comparison, ipso facto, denies the uniqueness of cultures and thus involves thought processes that desensitize one to the genuine reality of the cultures one studies. The second objection questions the possibility of comparative study. It says in effect that we cannot understand another culture or the past. When we assert that we do, all we really claim to know is our mental constructs of the other cultures or the past, because we cannot know something "we do not know that we do not know." The examination of this assertion would take us deep into epistemological questions that I do not wish to explore here.

One response to these two objections could be no different than Albert Camus's exclamation that silence is the best response to the absurdity of the universe! A more reasonable response would be the reiteration of the first point made in this chapter: human beings do compare; it is, therefore, necessary to examine how we compare in order to do it better. We know that complete uniqueness and universality are, by definition, outside the scope of comparative investigations. Comparison is possible only when we can apprehend both similarities and differences in the two or more phenomena we choose to study. The assumption that discretely different cultural phenomena have some similarity worth study is both defensible and justifiable on the grounds that human beings have been observed to respond to their material conditions and to other human beings in certain reasonably predictable patterns. It is these observations that led Murdoch, for example, to advance propositions such as: "Culture is learned, inculcated, social, ideational, gratifying, adaptive and integrative" (1940). Any generalization about cultures is in fact implicitly a comparative proposition whose limits and potentialities await explication.

PROBLEMS OF COMPARING CULTURAL ENTITIES

Scholars interested in comparative studies have attempted to minimize the force of the two objections briefly discussed above by being knowledgeable about and sensitive to the problems and pitfalls of comparing cultural entities.

What a scholar chooses to compare may well depend on personal interest, preparation in a discipline, cues from policy-making or research-granting agencies, one's knowledge of languages, the availability of primary and secondary materials, or access to the unit or area to be investigated. The choice of topics themselves may affect the extent of objectivity that a scholar can bring to an investigation. Awareness of this factor is highly desirable.

Comparative studies, like all studies, have an implicit or explicit frame of reference. It is necessary for a comparative social scientist to be as explicit as possible about this frame of reference. An explicit frame of reference will enable one to ask: has the theory, concept, indicator, etc. validity beyond a specific culture or duration? For example, Louis Dumont has asserted that the practice of caste in India is so uniquely a socio-religious phenomenon that considering it as a more extreme form of (economic) class or using the concept to explain racism in southern United States is invalid (Dumont 1970).

Ethnocentrism, namely, the tendency to evaluate the values, beliefs, attitudes, behaviors, etc. of another culture using the *apparently superior* criteria of one's own culture, is one of the landmines that a comparative investigator must learn to detect, and, as far as possible, avoid. For example, a dislike of Soviet-style communism may lead one to make errors of judgment about the reason Marxist and neo-Marxist theories and concepts appeal to liberation theologians in Latin America. Rudolph and Rudolph had this to say about one motivation that leads to ethnocentric evaluations:

> Occasionally one comes away from a colleague's work with the impression that he is reassuring himself and his readers of the uniqueness of the Western achievement, a uniqueness that would be endangered by recognition of the cultural, functional, and structural analogues to be found in non-Western traditional societies (1967, pp. 9–10).

An even more insidious pitfall is temperocentrism, the tendency to evaluate the past or predict the future on the basis of current preoccupations, perceptions, and recently evolved standards. Caste practices in India have been undergoing significant changes in the past two centuries; yet, one sometimes comes across claims about the meritocratic basis of dynamic class stratification processes in unfavorable contrast to a static depiction of the lack of social mobility in a caste-based society. (See Srinivas [1966] for one of his several discussions of Sanstritization and Westernization as group processes of social mobility in modern India.)

Ethnocentrism and temperocentrism can lead to the fallacy of retrospective determinism. While it is easy to prescribe their avoidance, we must acknowledge that complete avoidance of these tendencies is humanly impossible. One reason is that stipulative (specifies how certain words are to be used in a particular context) and programmatic (intentionally promotes the implementation of a course of action) terms often have ethnocentric and temperocentric biases built into them. Even if one were to avoid them in one's own work, one cannot detect, let alone deal with, all instances of these tendencies in the primary and secondary sources with which one works. One of the more common errors is projecting to a much larger group (Brazilian society), carefully delimited conclusions about a smaller group (slum dwellers in Recife) or processes. Another example: explanations of peasant resistance to particular "reforms" on grounds of conservatism may be indicative of nothing more than the urban bias of the author.

The terminology used in different cultures and by different scholars requires careful attention. Exaggerations and inconsistencies are, for example, endemic in the use of the term "democracy." Corporate capitalist and state socialist systems use the term "democracy" but they obviously mean entirely different things by it. Hence, it is extremely important to develop adequate definitions of the key terms and concepts used in a comparative study. Similarly, quantitative data in primary and secondary sources from different cultures may need adjustment and correction for duration and region before they become truly comparable. "Do not compare apples with oranges" is a common saying that, nevertheless, is one of the golden rules of comparative study.

Debates about the extent to which a scholar can be "value-free" or "value-neutral" in pursuing social scientific investigations have had their impact on discussions about comparative research. It is simply not possible for a scholar to be "value-free." The manner in which a question is asked (or a problem is posed) is grounded in value choices. A social scientist who claims to be value-free can only do so because he or she is either naive or dishonest. Implicitly or explicitly, comparisons deal with value positions on whether human nature is innately evil, neutral, or good; whether human beings ought to be subject to nature, be in harmony with it, or attain mastery over it; whether our time focus should be on the past, the present, or the future; whether our modal activity should be as beings, beings-in-becoming, or doing, and finally whether our relationship to each other should be lineal, collateral, or individualistic. (See Kluckhohn and Strodtbeck 1961, p. 12). "Value neutrality" as a stance one takes for particular periods of time on specific issues must, however, be encouraged. Eulau puts it well after pointing out that social scientists are hypersensitive to values because they are "increasingly involved in questions of social and public policy" (1968). Value neutrality, says Eulau, should be seen as having an instrumental character which implies its judicious use taking into account time and place:

> "Value neutrality"... serves to sensitize the behavioral scientist to the fact that he serves two masters: social values and scientific values. His science demands of him a maximum of truth and objectivity as means to scientific knowledge. Social purpose demands of him that he see to it that the consumers of his knowledge use it with a maximum of realism and rationality.... For I believe that the scientist's commitment to social purposes can best be implemented if he serves well the demands of science, and he can best serve the demands of science if he demonstrates judiciousness in regard to the multiple uses to which his scientific knowledge may be put (Eulau 1968, p. 167).

One way to display one's sensitivity to values in one's scholarly endeavors, in addition to practicing value neutrality within the process of inquiry, is to be explicit about one's value preferences which have informed one's choice of theoretical approaches. Perhaps the most defensible position with regard to the place of values in social scientific endeavors, in this connection, is that of Gunnar Myrdal:

> Quite apart from drawing any policy conclusions from social research or forming any ideas about what is desirable or undesirable, we employ and we need value premises in making scientific observations of facts and in analysing their causal interrelation. Chaos does not organize itself into any cosmos. We need viewpoints and they presume valuations. A "disinterested social science" is, from this viewpoint, pure nonsense. It never existed, and it will never exist. We can strive to make our thinking rational in spite of them, but only by facing the valuations, not by evading them (1953, p. 242).

> Value premises should be introduced openly. They should be explicitly stated and not kept hidden as tacit assumptions. They should be used not only as premises for our policy conclusions but also to determine the direction of our positive research.... This is, incidentally, our only protection against bias in research, for bias implies being directed by unacknowledged valuations. The value premises should be formulated as specifically and concretely as possible. They cannot be *a priori* self-evident or generally valid. They should be chosen, but not arbitrarily, for the choice must meet the criteria of relevance and significance to the actual society we are living in (1953, p. 241).

The present study of two social movements has several value premises. One is that, as Robert Redfield said, "Social science is not only a box of tools; it is also a light" (1947). One implication of the view that social science can be a light is that a social scientist must make choices about what to study and how the study is done. My decision to study Sarvodaya and Conscientization implies that the cultures of the "Third World" deserve to be respected; the progress of these cultures will be brought about mostly by people who belong to them; and that such progress must mean economic growth, the distribution of the results of economic growth especially to the poorest members of the society, and the creation of opportunities for everyone to participate in the political and cultural life of the society. Readers will detect other values in the formulation and discussion of issues and problems in these pages.

Barrington Moore, Jr., says:

> Though I do not think that the sole function of scholarship is utilitarian, yet why should we put our best energies into studying the past, or for that matter the present, if the results cannot serve somehow as a guide amid our perplexities and anxieties? (1956, p. 47).

The decision to study Sarvodaya and Conscientization was in part animated by the hope that it will clarify for me and the reader at least some of the issues that plague world development.

The attempt to promote objectivity often takes the form of stipulating elaborate procedures and methods. Formulation of hypotheses taking care to assure their validity (that what one measures is the real phenomenon one is investigating) and reliability (that one's results are stable over time), specification of independent and dependent variables, collection of reliable data, interpretation of these data using standard statistical manipulations, and, developing carefully circumscribed conclusions are some of these. This study, obviously, has not followed these formal social science procedures. The decision not to follow the formal methods of the social science is only partly the result of the conviction that such attempts do not necessarily assure objectivity. Indeed, some studies using the methods of hypothesis testing have yielded valuable insights (see Ramirez and Meyer 1980 for some of them). But many more studies have produced distorted and trivial results. The decision to pursue certain themes using primary and secondary sources was prompted in part by preference based on my perception of what I am best able to do and in part by the nature and the dimensions of the problem that interested me. The propositions discussed in the next chapter are conclusions of this study. But, with suitable modifications, they may become hypotheses that interest other scholars. The major concepts—that is, building blocks—which assisted me to erect the framework of propositions are: revitalization movements, values, social institutions, religion, revolution, reform, social structure, class, education, economy, and society. The intermediate (for example, praxis) and microlevel (for example, *ahimsa*) concepts are too numerous to mention here. The indexes provide a comprehensive list of them.

The availability of materials on, and the extent of access to, the phenomena under investigation may well determine the shape and tenor of conclusions. This too is a problem that a comparative scholar must deal with.

There is no shortcut to insights, based on thorough knowledge. Such knowledge, fortified by good judgment, should enable one to recognize that apparent similarities may sometimes conceal real differences (for example, similar institutional structures may not have similar functions; indeed, they may perform very different functions); also, the higher the level of abstraction one reaches in making a comparative statement, the greater is the likelihood of distortion. Good comparative studies cannot make predictions; they can provide reasonably valid and reliable syntheses and perspectives. Such syntheses and perspectives, at least, can promote cross-cultural dialogue on the presuppositions which animate the way members of different cultures think, feel, and act. Good comparative research is not unlike David K. Cohen and Michael S. Garet's description of applied or policy research. It

> resembles a discourse about social reality—a debate about social problems and their solutions. Like intelligent discussion or debate, [comparative] research does not necessarily reduce disagreement. Instead, it calls attention to the existence of conflicting positions, sometimes elaborates them and sometimes generates new issues altogether (1975, p. 42).

Ideal Comparisons and the Real World

The social scientific approach to comparison is derived from John Stuart Mill's (1873) five methods for identifying cause and effect (discussed in Mouly 1970, pp. 41-45).

1. *The method of agreement* postulates that "if two or more instances of the phenomenon under investigation have only one circumstance in common, the circumstance in which alone all the instances agree is the cause (or effect) of the given phenomenon."

2. *The method of difference* states that "if an instance in which the phenomenon under investigation occurs, and an instance in which it does not occur, have every circumstance save one in common, that one occurring only in the former; the circumstance in which alone the two instances differ, is the effect, or cause, or a necessary part of the cause, of the phenomenon."
3. *The joint method of agreement and disagreement* states that "if two or more instances in which the phenomenon occurs have only one circumstance in common, while two or more instances in which it does not occur have nothing in common save the absence of that circumstance; the circumstance in which alone the two sets of instances differ is the effect, or cause, or a necessary part of the cause, of the phenomenon."
4. *The method of residue* states that "subduct from any phenomenon such part as is known by previous inductions to be the effect of certain antecedents, and the residue of the phenomenon is the effect of the remaining antecedent."
5. *The method of concomitant variation* states that "whatever phenomenon varies in any manner whenever another phenomenon varies in some particular manner is either the cause or an effect of that phenomenon, or is connected with it through some fact of causation."

S. F. Nadel (1958) is certainly right in locating the comparative method as an extension of Mill's method of covariation as enunciated by Durkheim and others. Nadel points out that the method of co-variations presupposes three things: a preliminary hypothesis ("hunch") that phenomena A and B are related to each other in some significant and relevant way; social situations "are not made up of random items" but they reflect facts, attitudes, etc. which are meaningfully patterned in some kind of context; and a scholar cannot escape the responsibility of making judgments about these facts and patterns (1958, p. 224).

The basic formula is If A, then B.
                        If not A, then not B.
                        If A, then not B, etc.

Unit 1	*Unit 2*
If A, then B	If A, then B
C occurs	C does not occur
X, Y, Z explains the occurrence of C or	Absence of X, Y, Z explains C's non-occurrence

absence of *D, E, F*   *OR* Presence of *D, E, F* explains
explains *C*'s occurrence,   *C*'s non-occurrence, etc.
etc.

In ideally conducted comparative studies, there should be only two highly specific units that are under investigation and it should be possible to identify and measure every significant element or trait of these units and trace their changes under varying treatments or conditions. Such ideal studies can be conducted only in controlled laboratory conditions, that is, as observed experiments. Most comparative investigations use data or information gathered without the possibility of controlling the environment or the social context. In such situations, the specification is far less precise than, say, the frequency of responses a pigeon makes to a stimulus such as a measured amount of food in a laboratory. The units of study may range from an elementary school classroom to the value systems of cultural groups.

The listing of Mill's five canons and the reference to Nadel should not be construed as support for the view that in the social sciences we can eventually produce laws based on the isolation of cause-effect variables. Mill's canons make us acutely aware of the first point made in this chapter. Unconsciously and often we make comparative judgments based implicitly on the type of criteria Mill specifies. These criteria can provide us with guidelines for undertaking comparisons in non-laboratory situations.

We may identify three types of units for comparison. Examples of "system-type" units would be an urban school system or a peasant economy. The influence of a particular religion on a new social movement or policies for second language instruction at the secondary school level would be examples of "topic-type" units. Many system and topic-type units may focus on the solution of problems. If the emphasis is on the effectiveness of a newly introduced agricultural technique in a peasant economy or the success rate in second language examinations at the secondary level, we may say that they are "problem-type" units. These categories, of course, are not mutually exclusive and are primarily only of heuristic value. Most comparative studies are diachronic (the two or more units are similar in most respects except for the specific variables chosen for study) or synchronic (the two or more units vary greatly in most respects but occur at about the same time).

Comparisons using cardinal measures (since they imply no conscious evaluations between units studied) and those using ordinal measures (which do imply relative efficiency or effectiveness) can be undertaken in diachronic or synchronic modes. Comparisons undertaken for policy purposes obviously tend to favor procedures for establishing rank and preference. As such, comparisons in professional studies tend to have, at least implicitly, an ordinal perspective.

The study of Sarvodaya and Conscientization is a "problem-type" comparative study in that it hypothesizes that revitalization movements are attempts on the part of significant groups of people in a culture to develop a more satisfying culture which would eliminate several problems they perceive in the culture as it now exists. In terms of Sarana's types, this study may be characterized as a complete universe comparison because it attempts to deal comprehensively with a defined universe based on "inferential history." It has limited ability to generate synchronic generalizations and eschews ordinality.

The Steps Involved in Comparison

The careful construction of a frame of reference is absolutely crucial since the criteria by which comparative propositions and conclusions are reached tend to be imbedded in this frame of reference. It should, of course, be possible to modify this frame of reference on the basis of further evidence. The frame of reference for this study was established in Chapter 1 in the paragraph beginning with the sentence, "Revitalization movements necessarily imply the formulation and articulation of assertions about the relationships of human beings to each other and their material world." The frame of reference was given greater specificity by the decision to view Sarvodaya and Conscientization as cultural revitalization movements and by listing the eight major questions one may ask about these movements. These questions were modified, albeit in minor ways, during the course of research and writing. For example, the first list did not contain a question about the role of technology. Some of the other questions were phrased or grouped differently as I learned more about the movements themselves.

In certain comparative studies, it is extremely important to establish the time scale for comparison. In the case of this study, it was considered unnecessary to establish identical time periods. It seemed to me that comparisons of both movements would be, prima facie, justifiable on the grounds that they were near contemporaries. The Sarvodaya movement peaked in the late 1950s whereas the Conscientization movement in Brazil reached its zenith in the mid-1960s. Both movements continue to have adherents and proponents and thus continue to be contemporaries in some sense. Thus, the study is basically synchronic and cardinal in its approach.

The decision to study two *movements* left me no choice about whether the comparison would present a neat, static description of a very short time span (like a still photograph frozen in a moment of time) or the untidy, complex but more full description as well as analysis involving historical and other factors over several decades (like a cinematograph).

All social scientific endeavors studying social movements attempt to make statements about structural reality (for example, class) which correspond as closely as possible to the psychological reality of the people, movements, institutions, etc. that are investigated. Therefore, I chose to comparatively study Sarvodaya and Conscientization as complex, historical phenomena. This choice necessarily increased the risk of falling into any one of the pits outlined in a previous section. I hope, however, that the gains were worth the risks.

Brazil and India are nation-states. Although as a form of political organization it is no more than four centuries old, and there are many contemporary developments (for example, transnational corporations, political organizations, etc.) that are eroding their sovereignty, the nation-state is still the dominant political category within which many debates are conducted. This study simply acknowledges that fact for the two movements without making any case, as some scholars do, for the advantages of cross-national comparisons.

Should the attempt to compare social phenomena be strictly confined to the scholarly traditions of one well-defined discipline or should it be consciously inter-disciplinary? There can be no definitive *general* answer to that question. My decision to find answers to the eight major questions inevitably led me to seek answers where I could find them whether they be in philosophy, history, economics, educational studies, or anthropology. Thus, this study may be characterized as having a multi-disciplinary focus. It is, however, fair to add that my greater familiarity with anthropological as well as sociological theories and concepts is reflected in the choice of the framework and many of the detailed discussions.

In the rest of this chapter, I shall point to certain differences and similarities between the two movements by highlighting the differences between two of the men—Paulo Freire and Vinoba Bhave—associated with the two movements. Since there is some truth to the assertion that history is biography or that biography is history, we shall only refer to those biographical details which are relevant to this comparative study.

FREIRE AND BHAVE

Freire is a Brazilian, a *nordestino* (northerner), and a Roman Catholic; Bhave was an Indian, a Maharashtrian, and a Hindu. Freire knew poverty as a result of economic circumstances. Later in life, Bhave chose poverty as a way of life. Freire is a Brazilian of primarily Portuguese—which is to say European, colonial-extraction. Bhave was a native Indian.* Friere is an urban man; Bhave's roots were in the village. One is a loving husband, father of five children, and a doting grandfather. The other took a vow of celibacy at the age of ten. Freire enjoys the good things of life. In one of his talks, he referred to himself as a *biophile,* a lover of life. Bhave was an ascetic who ate only enough vegetables, fruits, nuts, and natural honey to keep himself alive and rigorously eschewed all stimulants and other "impurities" as part of his practice of *Samya-yoga* (to attain equanimity of mind, social equality and, finally, spiritual identity with the Supreme Being) (Bhave 1964, p. 1). He thus became a saint-politician, a unique Indian phenomenon. Freire, although considered a "below average" student, earned a doctor of philosophy degree and has had universities in many countries confer on him honorary doctorates. The other, although considered a brilliant student, gave up formal education at the age of twenty. Freire is the quintessential professor yearning—but not always able—to probe into and systematize his own thinking. Bhave was the quintessential *Karmayogi,* that is, man of disinterested action whose talks were often written up by his followers for publication. Since his exile, Freire has traveled by air and other available modes of transportation to many corners of the globe carrying the message of Conscientization. In Brazil, Freire was, for the most part, a petit-bourgeois reformer; in exile, and later in Brazil, he became a revolutionary being. Bhave chose not to pursue the possibility of study abroad but walked more than 40,000 miles (that is, 64,000 kilometers) in every part of India carrying the message of Sarvodaya. Although English is a foreign language to both of them, Freire's command of it is much greater than Bhave's.

I deliberately chose these items in extreme contrast first to make the point that comparison of the ethical philosophies these two men propagated is still possible.

Now let us consider some obvious similarities. Both Bhave and Freire have been put behind bars for opposing oppression and promoting freedom for poor people. But Freire was jailed by his own countrymen; Bhave was put in jail by a colonial government.

---

*Bhave died in 1982.

Although both Freire and Bhave are associated with the terms "Conscientization" and "Sarvodaya" respectively, neither of them coined these terms. But both Bhave and Freire infused their adopted terms with new meaning as they inductively dealt with concrete problems. Freire, like Bhave, has attributed many of the problems of his society to colonial rule and exploitation by the indigenous elites. They have both insisted that emancipation can only be achieved by individuals acting on their own or together in groups. Both Bhave and Freire are deeply religious men.

We shall consider other points of comparison in the next and concluding chapter.

10

THE DILEMMAS OF REVOLUTION THROUGH REFORM

> The money economy freed the individual from the dominance of the patriarchal authority, and enabled him to seek self-actualization through personal relationships of his own choosing.... Freedom from ancestral tradition also facilitated the rise of higher religious ideals which insisted on loyalty to the universal brotherhood of man, rather than to the immediate kinship group. The growth of the market had a twofold effect: it destroyed man's feelings of emotional, economic and spiritual security; but at the same time it established him as a rational person capable of free choice. It is the great task of the twentieth century to frame institutions which will restore man's feeling of rootedness without sacrificing the integrity of the individual.
>
> Desmonde, 1962, p. 179.

This chapter states in the form of propositions the comparative conclusions about Sarvodaya and Conscientization we may draw from the analyses in the preceding chapters. These propositions present my conclusions about issues that surfaced in this comparative study. They do not reiterate arguments and counterarguments that have been explored in previous chapters.

We shall discuss nine themes: revitalization movements as a third way for improving the material, cultural, and spiritual lives of people, particularly in the economically poor areas of the world; the ambivalent role of religion in such movements; the relative efficacy of violence and non-violence for promoting significant social change; the role of the state in promoting change; the necessity for genuine democracy; education as a process for improving the self-confidence of people as a first step to improving their lot in life; the constructive and destructive contribution of technology to human life; the message for affluent societies; and, the role of the individual.

Table 10-1 summarizes the approaches and answers of Sarvodaya and Conscientization to the questions implicit in each of the nine themes.

REVITALIZATION MOVEMENTS AS A THIRD WAY

It is exceedingly difficult to state categorically that all revolutions in the sense of cataclysmic, sudden upheavals that bring about changes in a society's relations of power are, prima facie, to be encouraged or discouraged. By definition, revolutions in this sense occur not because a scholar or a policy maker—or anyone, for that matter—recommends them, but because the participants in the revolution believe them to be necessary at that time. Whether nonparticipants perceive that belief to be irrational, unnecessarily costly, or very necessary is of practically no import to the participants. Moreover, as Robert Heilbroner (1967) and Barrington Moore, Jr. (1966, pp. 104, 509-23) have pointed out, most scholarly analyses ignore the structural violence that occur in society which prepare the ground for certain kinds of revolutions and thus tend to be blind to the emerging whirlwind. Says Heilbroner:

> I do not know how one measures the moral price of historical victories or how one can ever decide that a diffuse gain is worth a sharp and particular loss. I only know that the way in which we ordinarily keep the books of history is wrong. No one is now toting up the balance of the wretches who starve in India, or the peasants of Northeastern Brazil who live in the swamps on crabs, or the undernourished and permanently stunted children of Hong Kong or Honduras. Their sufferings go unrecorded, and are not present to counterbalance the scales when the furies of revolution strike down their victims. Barrington Moore has made a nice calculation that bears on this problem. Taking as the weight in one pan the 35,000 to 40,000 persons who lost their lives—mainly for no fault of theirs—as a result of the Terror during the French Revolution, he asks what would have been the death rate from preventable starvation and injustice under the *ancien regime* to balance the scales. "Offhand," he writes, "it seems unlikely that this would be very much below the proportion of .0010 which [the] figure of 40,000 yields when set against an estimated population of 24 million" (1967, p. 34).

It is, then, virtually impossible to approve or disapprove of revolutionary movements without considering their context.

Revitalization movements, as we pointed out in Chapter 1, are reform endeavors. Sarvodaya and Conscientization were reform

TABLE 10-1 SUMMARY COMPARISON OF SARVODAYA AND CONSCIENTIZATION

Problem, Issue, Theme	Sarvodaya in India	Conscientization in Brazil
	Gandhi, Bhave, and others developed their ethical notions in praxis.	Camara, Freire, and others developed their ethical notions in praxis.
Characterization of crisis in culture (as seen in evidence of increased individual stress, cultural distortion)	Problems of caste society accentuated by colonialism Inherent goodness of all human beings defeated by ignorance and warped social institutions.	Closed society created by colonialism Oppression of vast poor, powerless majority by wealthy powerful minority has created dehumanized beings.
Peak period of revitalization movement	circa 1950 to early 1960s	circa 1960 to 1965
Mazeway (people's images of nature, culture, personality, etc.) reformulation: elements	Individuals must pursue truth (satyagraha) and non-attachment	Individuals must discover and assert their uniqueness as human beings
	People must learn to govern themselves in society; the ideal form of government is that which governs the least. Hence, they must be in units of no more than 1,000 to 2,000 people.	It is impractical to do away with the state; the state's functions must be decentralized as much as possible; it must be responsive to the people. There is no inherent virtue in village-size government.
	While we must learn from other cultures, slavish imitation of other cultures is reprehensible.	As in Sarvodaya

TABLE 10-1 Continued

Problem, Issue, Theme	Sarvodaya in India	Conscientization in Brazil
	Courageous, active, non-violent resistance to evil is far superior to violent resistance to bring about desirable social change. The acceptance of self-suffering in the face of evil can lead to a change of heart in those who act unjustly.	While non-violent resistance to oppression is preferable to violence, a prior declaration that violence will never be used means that the oppressors will not take the demands of the oppressed seriously. There is no particular merit in self-imposed suffering, except as part of a multifaceted strategy.
	A society in which there is widespread poverty, disease, lack of access for a majority to education, decent housing, adequate clothing, and the arts is a structurally violent society.	As in Sarvodaya
	Truth is immutable, absolute. In the early stages of one's life, one needs material possessions and relationships to people to pursue truth. But one must develop a sense of detachment to the material world so that one can seek communion with Absolute Truth which is God.	Empirical truth is relative. There is no permanent objective reality since reality is shaped by the person's interaction with the material (non-human) and human world. So permanent critical consciousness is possible, necessary.

TABLE 10-1 Continued

Problem, Issue, Theme	Sarvodaya in India	Conscientization in Brazil
	There will always be wealthy and poor people in society. Society can benefit from permitting people to acquire wealth within limits. The wealthy must consider their wealth as a trust they hold for everyone. Such an attitude, fortified by everyone doing their own "bread labor," can virtually eliminate unjust behavior.	Great disparities in possession of, access to, wealth is prima facie evidence of injustice and oppression. It is foolhardy to think that the oppressors will, by exhortation, treat themselves as trustees of their wealth. The concept of "bread labor" is impractical.
	Large-scale industrialization and consequent urbanization dehumanizes people. We must encourage the development of only such technology that will make people feel, think, and act for the benefit of others. Retention of the human scale is imperative in economic and technological development. The fundamental criterion for technological development must be: will it increase the well-being of all? The profit motive must not be the driving	While, ideally, one cannot disagree with Sarvodaya's fundamental criterion, technological development cannot be consciously controlled by human beings. Such development is the consequence of dialectical interaction between persons, nature, and society. Whether a technique or an invention will be beneficial cannot be foreseen in many instances. Greater democratic participation and planning can help reduce or control

THE DILEMMAS OF REVOLUTION THROUGH REFORM / 121

TABLE 10-1 Continued

Problem, Issue, Theme	Sarvodaya in India	Conscientization in Brazil
	force of industrial and technological development.	some of the harmful consequences of industrialization and technological advancement. The profit motive must be kept in check.
	Education must not be "spoon-feeding of the masses."	Education must not be "banking."
	Knowledge must serve desirable spiritual and social goals.	As in Sarvodaya, because knowledge is not neutral.
	People must be involved in action programs to improve village sanitation, raise food production, promote cooperative movements, reduce illiteracy, etc. so that people can get the satisfaction of personal involvement in social change. Such activities will also increase their sense of capacity.	Heightening the consciousness of people about existing unjust social structures is far more important than promoting small-scale improvements. Small-scale improvements may postpone "the day of reckoning" for the oppressors.
	We must emphasize changing the hearts and minds of people and create opportunities for them to engage in actions that will help them practice a new way of life, a better society.	Any attempt to change people's attitudes and personal behaviors without a simultaneous attempt to confront individuals and elites who oppress people is romantic naiveté.

TABLE 10-1 Continued

Problem, Issue, Theme	Sarvodaya in India	Conscientization in Brazil
	Those who would promote constructive social change (i.e., leaders of the movement) must lead an exemplary life so that both their words and actions can have a persuasive influence.	It is far more important to take strategic and tactical decisions which would advance the cause of the oppressed than to be caught up in personal regimes of self-purification.
	The higher the civilization of a society the lesser will be its preoccupation with the acquisition and enjoyment of material goods. Its focus must be on social harmony and on provisions for the spiritual development of persons. People will learn to govern themselves well only if they learn to govern themselves, even badly, in the first instance. Therefore, the creation of autonomous village republics must begin immediately.	A society can focus on social harmony and spiritual development only if the economy is affluent enough to take care of the ordinary needs of its members. Thus material development must receive primacy in an economically poor society. Premature decisions to decentralize power will merely enable those in powerful positions to become even more entrenched. The particular form of government cannot be predetermined. It will have to be constructed after the seizure of power, by trial and error.
Communication and organization	Through *padayatra* (mission of walking) of Vinoba Bhave and	Through literacy classes for poor peasants and

TABLE 10-1 Continued

Problem, Issue, Theme	Sarvodaya in India	Conscientization in Brazil
	his requests for gifts of land, money, labor, intellect, etc. Speeches at meetings; publications of *Sarva Seva Sangth*.	workers. Speeches at meetings, particularly through church auspices; publications.
Adaptation	Bhave decided to present his views in a much more revolutionary socialistic vein. Yet, in its contacts with the general public the collective leadership chose to emphasize "trusteeship" instead of massive, non-violent, confrontation.	With the overthrow of the elected government in 1964, the movement withdrew into the church and became transformed as "base communities."
Cultural transformation	It is not possible to claim that Sarvodaya has visibly transformed Indian society.	As in India, so in Brazil.
Routinization	The crisis continues.	The crisis continues.

Source: Compiled by author.

movements. (In their reincarnations, they are still reform movements.) It is possible for those *not* directly involved in them to take a stance supporting or opposing them. Revitalization movements that assert that all human beings are worthy of respect, and that society's institutions must be recast to assure everyone, as far as humanly possible, equal opportunity and equal conditions to develop their potential for physical, social, and spiritual growth, deserve support. Such a stance implies a clear rejection of views that assert the inherent superiority of one race, ethnic group, social class, or gender over another. It also implies that any identifiable indigenous culture cannot be seen as inherently superior or inferior to other cultures. Every culture is in process of becoming because it is developed or destroyed by people. No culture is perfect, since it is imperfect human beings who construct the culture of their societies. The impetus to improve institutions and practices in a culture may have many (including foreign) origins, but the task of improvement can be undertaken effectively only by members of that culture. Whether revitalization movements—such as Sarvodaya and Conscientization—have succeeded in translating their visions into reality is exceedingly difficult to ascertain. Even if one concludes that their concrete efforts resulted in failures, they may have set in motion new movements to enlarge opportunities for more people to exercise more choice within certain constraints.

In the economically poor areas of Asia, Africa, and Latin America, revitalization movements have the potential to help the poor (who constitute the overwhelming majority) to recover their dignity because such movements begin with the premise that indigenous cultures, particularly of poor people, have validity and value. Attempts to cast these movements in terms of their affinity to Western perceptions about capitalism and communism constitute evidence of gross ethnocentrism and temperocentrism. These movements may take ideas from capitalism or communism but they must be viewed as indigenous attempts to solve their unique problems. This view, among other things, contains an implicit plea to the superpowers of the world to show greater understanding for such movements.

THE ROLE OF RELIGION IN REVITALIZATION MOVEMENTS

Institutionalized religions, more often than not, have been supporters of the political and economic elites. But, religion—understood as the quest to make some sense of a complex world, as an avenue to spiritual sources which provide people with courage in the midst of daunting difficulties, to find meaning for one's life, to transcend earthly existence—cannot be dismissed as mere superstition that the progress of science will eliminate. The failure of five decades of efforts in the Soviet Union to snuff out religion eloquently testifies to that fact. The religious inspiration, in its many manifestations, is known to have given otherwise unheroic men and women the strength to persevere in pursuing certain goals. The image of perfection and omnipotence that God (or any other synonym) represents in religion is also known to imbue many individuals who pursue such goals with a sense of self-discipline (which includes self-criticism) and humility (which includes respect for other persons). In this sense, religion can help safeguard everyone, particularly the leaders, in a revitalization movement from the corrosive effects of the corruptions and temptations of access to power. Furthermore, no movement to improve the conditions of life for people—including those which deny the existence of God—can function without a vision which transcends the present. That transcendence is ultimately a religious phenomenon.

The sorry fact that the religious quest is coopted or diverted by institutionalized religion is no mere aberration. It shows that as institutions, religious organizations are not much different from other institutions to the extent that they are organized and maintained by human beings. They thus take account of their material circumstances and their social context to ensure, at least, their survival and, at best, their expansion.

The implications for revitalization movements are obvious: they must challenge institutionalized religion to "go back to their roots." We have seen that both Sarvodaya and Conscientization have challenged many beliefs and practices, respectively, of Hinduism and Christianity. To be effective, part of that challenge must necessarily be directed at institutional structures and practices. Such challenges obviously carry risks. The extent to which revitalization movements can be effective will depend, in part, on the management of these risks.

VIOLENCE AND NON-VIOLENCE IN PROMOTING SOCIAL CHANGE

It is not just religious values and practices that revitalization movements—even religious revitalization movements—challenge. Significant questions about people's relationship to God, nature, and each other inevitably touch on economic, political, and myriad other cultural arrangements. If in some cases, it is affronts to widely held religious views that will trigger violent reactions, in other cases such reactions will result from challenges to concentrated ownership of private property or existing forms of dictatorship. If revitalization movements such as Sarvodaya and Conscientization are convinced about the justice of their challenges and, on principle, take the position that they will not initiate violence, they are immediately confronted with the issue of whether they should respond with violence to the violence of political and economic elites.

One part of the Sarvodaya answer is that the movement-adherent must consciously accept personal suffering as a self-purifying practice which will also have its beneficial effect on the adversary. The other part of the answer is that massive non-cooperation will bring the adversarial forces to their heel. The history of the Sarvodaya movement in India shows that, even in societies where parliamentary democracy is practiced, such prescriptions have not proven to be efficacious. The main reason is that most disciples and followers do not have the courage or the self-discipline to maintain a stance that puts such extreme pressure on their own patience, commitment, and lack of regard for personal well-being.

The experience of Conscientization raises other questions about the efficacy of non-violent methods in the face of extreme oppression of those who would challenge the status quo. The entire Sarvodaya strategy is based on the hope that, with a relatively short span of time, the adversary will either experience a conversion or will come to the conclusion that making some genuine concessions is less costly in the long run than reaping the whirlwind of massive non-cooperation. This view is based on the premise that all human beings are inherently good. Human actions compel one to lean to the view that the human heart is infinitely wicked and that those in power do not balk at indiscriminate and widespread murder of political adversaries. In such circumstances, revitalization movements do not have much choice but to accept the necessity of violence in certain circumstances. But, as they make that choice, they will have entered a process of transforming themselves *from* reform movements with revolutionary goals *to* revolutionary movements.

THE ROLE OF THE STATE

It is difficult to ignore the fact that the state, ultimately, can exist only because it has acquired implicit and explicit powers to coerce people. The Sarvodaya recognition of that fact leads it to advocate massive non-cooperation if warranted and the eventual elimination of the state to permit new forms of human cooperation. It is possible to read into the approach of Conscientization the Sarvodaya view that, gradually, the state would not be necessary as small-scale communities learn to govern themselves and to relate to other communities in loosely-knit federations.

The Sarvodaya position of not participating in electoral politics is not shared by the proponents of Conscientization. The Sarvodaya stance has only weakened the movement because the people to whom it directs its message see it as impractically irrelevant. Conscientization's effort to make the state more responsive in the first instance to the needs of people who are now ignored make it, paradoxically, a more genuine reform movement. The paradox stems from the fact that, unlike Sarvodaya, Conscientization acknowledges the necessity of violence in some circumstances.

THE NECESSITY FOR DEMOCRACY

As revitalization movements that emphasize the dignity and worth of the person, Sarvodaya and Conscientization proclaim certain values of democracy: every person should have the opportunity to participate in the crucial decisions that affect his or her life; persons who take and implement decisions should be accountable to those whose lives are significantly affected by them; economic and political units should make participation and accountability meaningful for people, and so on.

Both Sarvodaya and Conscientization, as movements, have not been able to fully show in their manner of organization how these democratic ideals can be put into practice. If one uses Wallace's threefold division of leader, disciples, and followers, one notices that as these movements became organized, communication gaps, misunderstandings, loss of morale, and other administrative problems have affected them. This statement is not meant to elicit surprise or condemnation. It is only meant to show that the problems of practicing democracy are immense; for example, bringing about a consensus concerning the costs to be borne for the benefits to be gained is not easy. The invention of effective techniques for ensuring democratic participation and true accountability can occur only after much trial and error, perhaps over a long period of time. Revitalization movements should not be expected to be immune from the problems of any organization that attempts to create new rules and regulations for human betterment.

EDUCATION'S ROLE

Formal or informal educational institutions are far more effective in transmitting the values, mores, and practices of a culture that already enjoys wide acceptance and has the approval of those in power than in transforming those values. It should, therefore, not surprise us that both Sarvodaya and Conscientization have had much difficulty in carrying out their educational mission. In institutional terms, formal education in the modern world can only have a supportive role: it can augment the efforts of the economic and political elites that establish the pace and direction of change in areas under their control. Yet, the processes of teaching and learning inevitably open up in people's minds questions about the contradictions implicit in the gaps between pretensions and practice in social institutions and whether, with or without divine help, human beings can create a more humane social order.

TECHNOLOGY IN THE SERVICE OF HUMANKIND

In the Sarvodaya movement, there was a deliberate attempt to create machines and techniques that would be labor-intensive and would enable people to be close to the production and consumption of goods and services. The dismal failure of that attempt to gain wide acceptance, except in certain model farms and workplaces, ought to give us pause.

Technological development is the result of the complex interaction of people to nature and is determined by people's needs and, sometimes, curiosity. Attempts to prevent such development even when the motivations are noble (as was undoubtedly the case in Sarvodaya) are not likely to succeed. Even if they do succeed in areas of Asia, Africa, and Latin America, it will indeed be a Pyrrhic victory: in view of the systemic, international nature of today's world, these areas will then be forced to be permanent "hewers of wood and drawers of water" for the more developed areas of the world.

Many technological developments have been beneficial to humankind; many have not. It is not possible, in this as in almost any other field of human endeavor, to have only good outcomes and, somehow, eliminate harmful ones. Safeguards that ensure accountability and enlightened public opinion can reduce the extent of harm. It is to these matters that revitalization movements should address themselves.

THE MESSAGE FOR AFFLUENT SOCIETIES

We shall resist the temptation to dwell on certain obvious and important messages such as that the affluent societies have an obligation to help economically poorer societies, or, that some people in affluent societies must choose to practice a less wasteful lifestyle to protect the total resources of planet Earth, or, that if they would only listen and learn, people in affluent societies can learn much from the rich heritage of societies that are now, but were not always, poor.

Instead, let us mention just one matter. The experience of wealthy individuals from the beginning of civilization and, more recently, the experience of wealthy societies shows clearly that while a certain measure of material well-being is a necessary condition for most people to strive for happiness, material wealth in itself does not ensure personal fulfillment or social harmony. We know very little about how to define genuine and other types of needs for persons and societies, the mechanisms that stimulate the creation of new needs, the manner in which the processes of need fulfillment for some people lead to the deprivation of many more others, and so on. At least some enlightened groups in affluent societies might be persuaded to examine with people in poorer societies the limits and possibilities of "needs definition" that transcend cultural boundaries and hold the potential for the true pursuit of happiness.

THE ROLE OF THE INDIVIDUAL

It is fitting, perhaps, that this chapter and this book should conclude on this note. It is possible to charge that one has finally nothing more original to say than that individuals must take their destiny in their hands. I do not assert that, since I fully agree with both elements of Marx and Engel's view that individuals do make their history but that they do not do so in circumstances of their choice. Revitalization movements such as Sarvodaya and Concientization recognize both of these elements to varying degrees.

Can reform movements such as Sarvodaya and Concientization attain revolutionary goals? The evidence we have examined compels us to conclude that they cannot do so, if we accept Crane Brinton's definition of revolution in Chapter 1. But reform movements that address concrete problems with specific proposals set in a disciplined vision of a more humane social order do make it possible for many people to assert to themselves and to others—as they had not done before—that they are worthwhile persons. The possibilities that arise from that simple assertion can have significant consequences in the long run. Even in their apparent failure in the short term, genuine reform movements are optimistic testaments. They beckon us to struggle for the improvement of human beings and of human institutions.

BIBLIOGRAPHY

Ashe, Geoffrey. 1968a. "Can Nonviolence Change Society?" *Gandhi Marg,* vol. 12, no. 3 (July): 345-61.
──. 1968b. *Gandhi: A Study in Revolution.* London: Heinemann.
Babin, Jacques. 1975. "Interview with Violent Pacifist Liberation Man of God—Dom Helder Camara." *Cooperation Canada* 20 (May): 3-9.
Banerji, J. 1973. *Mao-Tse Tung and Gandhi: Perspectives on Social Transformation.* Bombay: Allied.
Barnard, Clift. 1980. "Imperialism, Underdevelopment and Education." In *Literacy and Revolution: The Pedagogy of Paulo Freire,* edited by Robert Mackie. London: Pluto Press.
Barndt, Deborah. 1980. *Education and Social Change: A Photographic Study of Peru.* Dubuque, Iowa: Kendall/Hunt.
Bhattacharya, Buddhadeva. 1969. *Evolution of the Political Philosophy of Gandhi.* Calcutta: Calcutta Book House.
Bhattacharya, Sabyasachi. 1966. "Cultural and Social Constraints on Technological Innovation and Economic Development: Some Case Studies." *Indian Economic and Social History Review,* vol. 3, no. 3 (September): 240-67.
Bhave, Vinoba. 1964. *Revolutionary Sarvodaya.* Bombay: Bharatiya Vidya Bhavan.
──. 1959. *Thoughts on Education.* Trans. Marjorie Sykes. 2nd ed. Kashi: Sarva Seva Sangh Prakashan.
──. 1958. *Sarvodaya and the Business Community.* Compiled by Donald G. Groom. Tanjore: Sarvodaya Prachuralaya.
──. 1957. *Sarvodaya and Communism.* Tanjore: Sarvodaya Prachuralaya.
Bondurant, Joan V. 1965. *Conquest of Violence: The Gandhian Philosophy of Conflict.* Rev. ed. Berkeley and Los Angeles: University of California Press.
Bottomore, T.B., ed. 1964. *Karl Marx: Early Writings.* Trans. T.B. Bottomore. New York: McGraw-Hill.

Bose, N.K. 1948. *Selections from Gandhi.* Ahmedabad: Navajivan.

Bowers, C.A. 1983. "Linguistic Roots of Cultural Invasion in Paulo Freire's Pedagogy." *Teachers College Record,* vol. 84, no. 4 (Summer): 935-53.

Brinton, Crane. [1952] 1960. *The Anatomy of Revolution.* Rev. ed. New York: Vintage Books.

Broucker, Jose de. 1979. *Dom Helder Camara, The Conversations of a Bishop: An Interview with Jose de Broucker.* Trans. Hilary Davies. London: Collins.

Bruneau, Thomas C. 1980. "The Catholic Church and Development in Latin America: The Role of the Basic Christian Communities." *World Development,* vol. 8, no. 7/8 (July/August): 535-44.

―――. 1974. *The Political Transformation of the Brazilian Catholic Church.* London: Cambridge University Press.

Cabral, Amilcar. 1973. "The Role of Culture in the Battle for Independence." *Unesco Courier* (November): 12-16ff.

Camara, Dom Helder. 1971. *Revolution Through Peace.* Trans. from Portuguese *"Revolucao Dentro da Paz,"* by Amparo McLean, 1968. New York: Harper and Row.

Cameron, James. 1974. *An Indian Summer.* London: Macmillan.

Cohen, David K., and Michael S. Garet. 1975. "Reforming Educational Policy with Applied Research." *Harvard Educational Review,* vol. 45, no. 1 (February): 17-43.

Coles, Robert. 1981. "Children of a Brazilian Favela." *Harvard Educational Review,* vol. 51, no. 1 (February): 79-84.

Collins, Denis E. 1977. *Paulo Freire: His Life, Work and Thought.* New York: Paulist Press.

Dandavate, Madhu. 1977. *Marx and Gandhi.* Bombay: Popular Prakashan.

Das Gupta, V. 1969. "Gandhi on Social Conflict." In *Gandhi: Theory and Practice, Social Impact and Contemporary Relevance: Proceedings of a Seminar,* edited by S.C. Biswas. Simla: Indian Institute of Advanced Study: 31-35.

de Kadt, Emmanuel. 1970. *Catholic Radicals in Brazil.* London: Oxford University Press.

Desai, Mahadev. 1953. *The Gospel of Selfless Action or the Gita According to Gandhi.* Ahmedabad: Navajivan.

de Silva, G.V.S., N. Mehta, A. Rahman, and P. Wignaraja. 1979. "Bhoomi Sena: A Struggle for People's Power." *Gandhi Marg,* vol. 1, no. 1 (new series) (April): 73-86.

Desmonde, William H. 1962. *Magic, Myth, and Money: The Origin of Money in Religious Ritual.* New York: The Free Press of Glencoe.

Dewitt, John Jefferson. 1971. "An Exposition and Analysis of Paulo Freire's Radical Psycho-Social Andragogy of Development." Ed.D. diss., Boston University.

Dhanagre, D.N. 1975. *Agrarian Movements and Gandhian Politics.* Agra: Agra University Institute of Social Sciences.

Doctor, Adi H. 1967. *Sarvodaya: A Political and Economic Study.* New York: Asia.

―――. 1964. *Anarchist Thought in India.* Bombay: Asia.

Dumont, Louis. 1970. *Religion, Politics and History in India: Collected Papers in Indian Sociology.* The Hague: Mouton.

Elias, John L. 1976. *Conscientization and Deschooling: Freire's and Illich's Proposals for Reshaping Society.* Philadelphia: Westminster Press.

———. "Adult Literacy Education in Brazil—1961-1964: Metado Paulo Freire." *Canadian and International Education,* vol. 2, no. 1 (June): 67-84.

Eulau, Heinz. 1968. "Values and Behavioral Science: Neutrality Revisited." *Antioch Review,* vol. 28, no. 2 (Summer): 160-67.

Ewert, Merrul D. 1981. "Proverbs, Parables and Metaphors: Applying Freire's Concept of Codification in Africa." *Convergence,* vol. 14, no. 1: 73-44.

Fersh, Seymour. 1978. *Asia: Teaching About/Learning From.* New York: Teachers College (Columbia University) Press.

Fraser, Stewart E., and William B. Brickman. 1968. *A History of International and Comparative Education: Nineteenth Century Documents.* Glenview, Ill.: Scott, Foresman.

Freire, Paulo. 1981. "The People Speak Their Word: Learning to Read and Write in Sao Tome and Principe." *Harvard Educational Review,* vol. 51, no. 1 (February): 27-30.

———. 1978. *Pedagogy in Process: The Letters to Guinea-Bissau.* London: Writers and Readers Publishing Cooperative.

———. 1973a. "Education, Liberation and the Church." SE/38, *Study Encounter,* vol. 9, no. 1: 1-16.

———. 1973b. *Education for Critical Consciousness.* New York: Seabury Press.

———. 1970. "Cultural Freedom in Latin America." In *Human Rights and the Liberation of Man in the Americas,* edited by Louis M. Colonnese. Notre Dame, Indiana: University of Notre Dame Press: 162-79.

Friedman, Norman L. 1967. "Nativism." *Phylon,* vol. 28, no. 4: 408-15.

Furtado, Celso. 1963. *The Economic Growth of Brazil: A Survey from Colonial to Modern Times.* Berkeley: University of California Press.

Galtung, Johann. 1980. *The True Worlds: A Transnational Perspective.* New York: Free Press.

Gandhi, Mohandas K. 1964. *All Are Equal in the Eyes of God* (Selections from Mahatma Gandhi). New Delhi: Publications Division.

———. 1952. *Rebuilding Our Villages.* Ed. Bharatan Kumarappa. Ahmedabad: Navajivan.

———. 1940. *An Autobiography: The Story of My Experiments with Truth.* 2nd ed. Trans. Mahadev Desai. Ahmedabad: Navajivan.

———. 1930. *Mahatma Gandhi: His Own Story.* Ed. C.F. Andrews. New York: Macmillan.

Goulet, Denis. 1971. *The Cruel Choice: A New Concept in the Theory of Development.* New York: Atheneum.

Grabowski, Stanley M., ed. 1972. *Paulo Freire: A Revolutionary Dilemma for the Adult Educator.* Occasional Papers No. 32. Syracuse: Publications in Continuing Education.

Hare, Paul A., and Herbert H. Blumberg, eds. 1977. *Liberation Without Violence: A Third Party Approach.* London: Rex Collings.

Harris, Marvin. 1974. *Cows, Pigs, Wars and Witches: The Riddle of Culture.* New York: Random House.

Heilbroner, Robert L. 1967. "Counterrevolutionary America." *Commentary,* vol. 43, no. 4 (April): 31-38.

Hellman, John. 1981. *Emmanuel Mounier and the New Catholic Left, 1930-1950.* Toronto: University of Toronto Press.

Hetten, Bjorn, and Gordon Tomm. 1971. "The Development Strategy of Gandhian Economics." *Journal of Indian Anthropology Society* 6: 51-66.

Hiller, Harry H. 1977. "Internal Problem Resolution and Third Party Emergence." *Canadian Journal of Sociology,* vol. 2, no. 1 (Winter): 55-75.

Hoffman, Daniel. 1961. *India's Social Miracle: The Story of Acharya Vinoba Bhave and His Movement for Social Justice and Cooperation, along with a Key to America's Future and the Way for Harmony between Man, Nature and God.* Healdsburg, Calif: Nuturegraph.

India, Government of. 1979. *The Collected Works of Mahatma Gandhi.* Vol. 75 (October 11, 1941-March 31, 1942). Delhi: Publications Division.

India, Ministry of Education. 1959. *Syllabus for Basic Schools.* Delhi: Publications Division.

———. 1956. *Report of the Assessment Committee on Basic Education.* Delhi: Publications Division.

Iyer, Raghavan N. 1973. *The Moral and Political Thought of Mahatma Gandhi.* New York: Oxford University Press.

Jesudasan, S.J., Ignatius. 1984. *A Gandhian Theology of Liberation.* New York: Mary Knoll.

Kantowsky, Detlef. 1980. *Sarvodaya: The Other Development.* Bombay: Vikas.

Kher, V.B., ed. 1957. *Economic and Industrial Life and Relations.* Compilation of M.K. Gandhi's writings, vols. 1, 2, 3. Amhedabad: Navajivan.

Kidd, Ross, and Krishna Kumar. 1981. "Co-opting Freire: A Critical Analysis of Pseudo-Freirean Adult Education." *Economic and Political Weekly,* vol. 16, nos. 1, 2 (January 3-10): 27-36.

Kluckhohn, Florence R., and Fred L. Strodtbeck. 1961. *Variations in Value Orientations.* Evanston, Ill.: Harper and Row.

Koshy, Ninan, ed. 1975. *Education for Liberation: Addresses by Paulo Freire and Critical Reflections on Indian Education.* Bangalore: Ecumenical Christian Centre.

Kurien, C.T. 1974. *Poverty and Development.* Madras: Christian Literature Society.

LADOC. 1974. "The LADOC 'Keyhole' Series: Latin Americans Look into Their Social and Religious Problems." Washington, D.C.: USCC, Division of Latin America.

Lanza del Vasto, Joseph Jean. [1954] 1974. *Gandhi to Vinoba: The New Pilgrimage.* Trans. from the French by Philip Leon. New York: Schocken.

LeVine, Robert. 1963. "Political Socialization and Cultural Change." In *Old Societies and New States,* edited by Clifford Geertz. New York: Free Press: 280-303.
Marriott, Mckim. 1952. "Technological Change in Overdeveloped Rural Areas." *Economic Development and Cultural Change,* vol. 1, no. 3: 261-72.
Mashruwala, Kishorlal. 1951. *Gandhi and Marx.* Introduction by Vinoba Bhave. Ahmedabad: Navajivan.
Mathur, Jagannath Swarup. 1971. *Industrial Civilization and Gandhian Economics.* Allahabad: Pustakayan.
Matthews, Michael. 1980. "Knowledge, Action and Power." In *Literacy and Revolution: The Pedagogy of Paulo Freire,* edited by Robert Mackie. London: Pluto Press.
McLaughlin, Elizabeth T. 1974. *Ruskin and Gandhi.* Lewisburg, Pa.: Bucknell University Press.
Mehta, Ved. 1976. *Mahatma Gandhi and His Apostles.* New York: Penguin Books.
Merton, Thomas. 1965. *Gandhi on Non-Violence.* New York: New Directions.
Mies, Maria. 1973. "Paulo Freire's Method of Education: Conscientization in Latin America." *Economic and Political Weekly* (Bombay), vol. 8, no. 39 (September 29): 1764-67.
Miller, Robert William. 1960. "The Dilemma of Middle-Class Pacifism." *Gandhi Marg,* vol. 4, no. 4 (October): 295-304.
Mookerjee, Girija K. 1967. *The Indian Image of Nineteenth Century Europe.* Bombay: Asia.
Mookherji, S.B. 1961. "Gandhi and Marx: Some Basic Differences." *Gandhi Marg,* vol. 5, no. 3 (July): 221-33.
Moore, Jr., Barrington. 1966. *Social Origins of Dictatorship and Democracy: Lord and Peasant in the Making of Modern Society.* Boston: Beacon Press.
―――. 1956. "Strategy in Social Science." In *Political Power and Social Theory: Six Studies.* Cambridge, Mass.: Harvard University Press: ch. 4.
Mouly, George J. 1970. *The Science of Educational Research.* 2nd ed. New York: D. Van Nostrand.
Mounier, Emmanuel. 1952. *Personalism.* Trans. Philip Mairet. Notre Dame, Indiana: University of Notre Dame Press.
"M.R." 1972. "The Naxalie-Sarvodaya Syndrome: The Patnaik Case." *Economic and Political Weekly,* vol. 7, no. 16 (April 15): 793-94.
Mukerjee, Hirendranath. 1979. *Gandhiji: A Study.* 3rd rev.ed. New Delhi: People's Publishing.
Mukherjee, Subrata. 1979. "Marx and Gandhi: A Comparison." *Gandhi Marg,* vol. 1, no. 7 (New Series) (October): 399-415.
Muller, Friederich Max. 1899. *India: What Can It Teach Us?* 2nd ed. London: Longmans, Green. A course of lectures delivered before the University of Cambridge.
Mumford, Lewis. 1967. *The Myth of the Machine: Technics and Human Development.* New York: Harcourt, Brace, and World.
―――. 1934. *Technics and Civilization.* New York: Harcourt, Brace.

Murdoch, George Peter. 1940. "The Cross-Cultural Survey." *American Sociological Review,* vol. 5, no. 3 (June): 361-70.
Myrdal, Gunnar. 1953. "The Relation Between Social Theory and Social Policy." *British Journal of Sociology* 4 (September): 210-42.
Nadel, S.F. [1951] 1958. "Experimental Anthropology." In *Foundations of Social Anthropology,* ch. 9. London: Cohen and West.
Naess, Arne. 1974. *Gandhi and Group Conflict: An Exploration of Satyagraha, Theoretical Background.* Oslo: Universitets-forlaget.
Narayan, Shriman, ed. 1969. *The Voice of Truth: Selections from the Writings and Speeches of Gandhi.* Ahmedabad: Navajivan.
Nayyar, Dev Prakash. 1952. *Building for Peace or Gandhi's Ideas on Social (Adult) Education.* Delhi: Atma Ram.
Niedergang, Marcel. 1980. "Brazil's Northeast: Invasion of the Favelados." *Guardian Weekly,* November 2, 1980, p. 12.
Oommen, T.K. 1981. "Gandhi and Village: Towards a Critical Appraisal." *Gandi Marg,* vol. 2, no. 10 (January): 588-95.
―――. 1979. "Rethinking Gandhian Approach." *Gandhi Marg,* vol. 1, no. 7 (October): 416-23.
―――. 1972. *Charisma, Stability and Change: An Analysis of the Bhoodan-Gramdan Movement in India.* New Delhi: Thomson Press.
Ostergaard, Geoffrey, and Melville Currell. 1971. *The Gentle Anarchists: A Study of the Leaders of the Sarvodaya Movement for Non-Violent Revolution in India.* Oxford: Clarendon Press.
Page, Joseph A. 1972. *The Revolution That Never Was: Northeast Brazil, 1955-1964.* New York: Grossman.
Patel, M.S. 1956. *The Educational Philosophy of Mahatma Gandhi.* Ahmedabad: Navajivan.
Priest, T.A. 1960. "The Concept of Sarvodaya in Gandhian Education." *Educational Theory,* vol. 10, no. 2 (April): 148-60.
Radcliffe, David. 1979. "Sarvodaya and the Western World." *Canadian and International Education,* vol. 8, no. 1: 62-74.
Ram, Rattan. 1972. *Gandhi's Concept of Political Obligation.* Calcutta: Minerva Associates.
Ram, Suresh. 1962. *Vinoba and His Mission: Being an Account of the Rise and Growth of the Bhoodan Yajna Movement.* 3rd ed. Rajghat, Kashi: Akhil Bharat Sarva Seva Sangh.
Ramirez, Francisco O., and John W. Meyer. 1980. "Comparative Education: The Social Construction of the Modern World System." *American Review of Sociology* 6: 369-99.
Randall, Margaret. 1983. *Christians in the Nicaraguan Revolution.* Vancouver: New Star Books.
Redfield, Robert. 1947. "The Social Uses of Social Science." *University of Colorado Bulletin* 47 (May 24): 1-8.
Richards, Glyn. 1982. *The Philosophy of Gandhi: A Study of His Basic Ideas.* New York: Barnes & Noble.
Rolnick, P.J. 1962. "Charity, Trusteeship and Social Change in India." *World Politics,* vol. 14, no. 3 (November): 439-60.
Rudolph, Lloyd S., and Susanne Hoeber Rudolph. 1967. *The Modernity of*

Tradition: Political Development in India. Chicago: University of Chicago Press.
Sachchidananda et al. 1976. *Sarvodaya and Development: Multi-disciplinary Perspectives from Musahari.* Patna: A.N.S. Institute of Social Studies.
Sale, Kirkpatrick. 1980. *Human Scale.* New York: G.P. Putnam's Sons.
Sapir, E. 1924. "Culture, Genuine and Spurious." *American Journal of Sociology* 19 (January): 401-29.
Sarana, Gopala. 1975. *The Methodology of Anthropological Comparisons.* Tucson, Arizona: The University of Arizona Press.
Sarva Seva Sangh. 1973. *Challenge of Poverty and the Gandhian Answer.* Rajghat, Varanasi: Sarva Seva Sangh Prakashan.
Schumacher, E.F. 1973. *Small Is Beautiful: A Study of Economics as if People Mattered.* London: Blond and Briggs.
———. 1968. "Buddhist Economics." *Resurgence* (London), vol. 1, no. 11: 1-4.
Sethi, J.D. 1977. "Theories of Technical Progress: Neo-Classical, Keynesian, Marxian and Gandhian." *Gandhi Marg,* vol. 21, no. 2 (April): 122-40.
Shah, C.G. 1963. *Marxism, Gandhism, Stalinism.* Bombay: Popular Prakashan.
Sharma, B.S. 1960. "The Philosophical Basis of Sarvodaya." *Gandhi Marg,* vol. 4, no. 3 (July): 258-62.
Sik, Ota. 1976. *The Third Way: Marxist-Leninist Theory and Modern Industrial Society.* Trans. Marian Sling. New York: International Arts and Sciences Press.
Singer, Milton. 1972. *When a Great Tradition Modernizes: An Anthropological Approach to Indian Civilization.* New York: Praeger.
Singh, R.P. 1979. *Education in an Imperial Colony.* New Delhi: National.
Sinha, Archana. 1978. *The Social and Political Philosophy of Sarvodaya.* Patna: Janaki Prakashan.
Sivaraksa, Sulak. 1980. "Buddhism and Development: Is Small Beautiful?" *Gandhi Marg,* vol. I (New Series), no. 12 (March): 765-79.
Sohn-Rethel, Alfred. 1978. *Intellectual and Manual Labour: A Critique of Epistemology.* Atlantic Heights, N.J.: Humanities Press.
Spring, Joel. 1975. *A Primer of Libertarian Education.* New York: Free Life Editions.
Srinivas, M.N. 1966. *Social Change in Modern India.* Berkeley: University of California Press.
Srinivasa, Inguva. 1971. *Gandhi and Development Theory: An Inquiry into the Economic Philosophy of Mahatma Gandhi Vis-a-vis Modern Western Theory of Economic Development.* Machilipatnam: I.S. Publishers.
Tandon, Vishwanath. 1980. "Vinoba and Satyagraha." *Gandhi Marg,* vol. 2 (New Series) no. 7 (October): 385-94.
Tendulkar, D.G. 1960. *Mahatma.* 8 vols. Vol. 4. New ed., rev. 1960-63. Delhi: Publications Division.
Thirta, N.V. 1959. "A Comparative Study of Gandhi's Educational Ideas

and the Government of India's Basic Education Programs—A Study in Values." Ph.D. diss., Stanford University.

Torres, Carlos Alberto. 1982. "From the 'Pedagogy of the Oppressed' to "A Luta Continua': An Essay on The Political Pedagogy of Paulo Freire." *Education With Production,* vol. 1, no. 2 (November): 76-97.

Wallace, Anthony F.C. 1961. "Schools in Revolutionary and Conservative Societies." In *Anthropology and Education,* edited by Frederick C. Gruber. Philadelphia: University of Pennsylvania Press: 25-54.

———. 1956. "Revitalization Movements: Some Theoretical Considerations for Their Comparative Study." *American Anthropologist,* vol. 58, no. 2 (April): 264-81.

Wallace, Anthony F.C., and John Atkins. 1960. "The Meaning of Kinship Terms." *American Anthropologist,* vol. 62 (February): 58-80.

Wallerstein, Immanuel. 1979. *The Capitalist World—Economy.* Cambridge: Cambridge University Press.

Yuille-Smith, C.R. 1980. "The Western Idea of Reincarnation and Karma." *Gandhi Marg,* vol. 1 (New Series) no. 10 (January): 660-65.

Zachariah, Mathew. 1984. "The Berger Commission Inquiry Report and the Revitalization of Indigenous Cultures." *Canadian Journal of Development Studies,* vol. 5, no. 1: 65-77.

———. 1981. *Christian Education and Cultural Transformation in India.* Madras: The Christian Literature Society.

———. 1979. "Presidential Address: Comparative Educators and International Development Policy." *Comparative Education Review,* vol. 23, no. 3 (October): 341-54.

Zachariah, Mathew, and Arlene Hoffman. 1985. "Gandhi and Mao on Manual Labour in the School: A Retrospective Analysis." *International Review of Education* 31 (August).

NAME INDEX

Barnard, Clift, 30
Barndt, Deborah, 38
Bhattacharya, Buddhadeva, 21
Bhattacharya, Sabyasachi, 95
Bhave, Vinoba, 9, 11, 15, 18; as Ghandi's spiritual heir, 23, 24, 41, 42, 43, 73, 84, 114
Bondurant, Joan V., 16, 17
Bottomore, T.B., 64
Bowers, C.A., 100-01
Brinten, Crane, 1
Bruneau, Thomas C., 32, 39, 49, 53

Cabral, Amilcar, 2
Camara, Dom Helder, 28, 50-51
Cameron, James, 90
Cohen, David K. and Michael S. Garet, 109

Dandavate, Madhu, 87
Dandekar, V.M. and Rath, N., 5
Das Gupta, A.K., 97-98
de Kadt, Emmanuel, 29, 32-33, 50, 53, 76
Dewitt, John Jefferson, 29, 53-54
Doctor, Adi H., 16, 17-18, 22, 64, 96
Dumont, Louis, 105
Dutt, R.C., 22

Elias, John L., 32, 33
Eulau, Heinz, 106-07
Ewert, Merrul D., 100

Freire, Paulo, 9, 11, 31, 34-35, 37, 51-53, 68, 73, 75-76
Freyer, Gilberto, 29

Gandhi, Mohandus K., 9, 11, 13, 16, 17-18, 22, 45, 57, 69-70, 83-84, 85
Goulet, Denis, 9-10

Harris, Marvin, 95
Heilbroner, Robert L., 117
Hellman, John, 53
Hoffman, Daniel, 96

Iyer, Raghvan N., 13, 17, 44

Johnson, Donald, 103

Kher, V.B., 21
Kidd, Ross, 100
Kurien, C.T., 5

Lanza del Vasto, Joseph Jean, 23-24, 25, 26
LeVine, Robert, 3

Marriott, McKim, 95
Mashruwala, Kishorlal, 57, 58-59, 60
Matthews, Michael, 78
McLaughlin, Elizabeth T., 17
Mehta, Ved, 18
Merton, Thomas, 82

Mies, Maria, 32, 35-36
Mill, John Stuart, 109-10, 111
Miller, Robert William, 98
Mookherjee, Girija K., 56
Mookherji, S.B., 60
Moore, Barrington, Jr., 108, 117
Mounier, Emmanuel, 36-37, 53
Mukerjee, Hirendranath, 59
Mumford, Lewis, 81
Murdoch, George Peter, 104
Myrdal, Gunner, 107

Nadel, S.F., 110
Naess, Arne, 18-19
Narayan, Shiman, 20, 47, 61
Nayyar, Dev Prakash, 71
Nehru, Jawaharlal, 15

Oomman, T.K., 87, 97
Ostergaard, Geoffrey and Melville Currell, 12, 20, 22

Ram, Suresh, 43, 92
Ramirez, Francisco O. and Meyer, John W., 108
Randall, Margaret, 55
Redfield, Robert, 107-08

Rolnick, P.J., 63-64
Rudolph, Lloyd S. and Rudolph, Susanne Hoeber, 3, 105

Sachchidananda, et al., 61, 92-93
Samantabhadra, 16
Sapir, E., 40
Schumacher, E.F., 84, 87
Sharma, B.S., 18, 45
Sik, Ota, 82-83, 89
Singer, Milton, 42
Sohn-Rethel, Alfred, 94
Spring, Joel, 75
Srinivas, M.N., 105

Tendulkar, D.G., 69
Thirta, N.V., 71-72
Thoreau, Henry David, 17, 63, 102
Tolstoy, Leo, 17

Vaz, de Lima Henrique, 28

Wallace, Anthony F.C., 4, 5, 6, 7, 8, 9, 41, 80, 127
Wallerstein, Immanuel, 2

Yuille-Smith, C.R., 86

SUBJECT INDEX

Brazil: Agresta, 30; Massapa, 30; patriarchal organization of the family, 29; Recife, 30; Roman Catholics in, 49

Brazil, colonization: abolition of slavery, 31; agrarian and exporting societies, 29; closed society, 29, 31, 79; domination of Spain and Portugal, 29, 30; economic structures of conquerors, 29; economy upon slave labor—Negroes, 29; feudal system, 29; foreign markets, 29; large landowners, 30; rural oligarchy, 29; sugar plantation as foundation of new economy, 29; transplantation by invaders, 29

Brazil, developing: agricultural and other reforms, 31; communist influence, 32; Freire's literacy campaign, 31; Goulart's reform efforts, 31; Movimento de Cultura Popular, 31; northeastern region, 30; Peasants Leagues (ligas camponesas), 31; Superintendency for the Development of the Northeast (SUDENE), 31-32; union organization, 31

Brazil, problems: degeneration of social fabric, 30; peasants and worker, 50, 55; eligibility for franchise, 59; food cultivation onto marginal land, 56; forest destruction, 30; slumdwellers in Recife, 199; urban decay, 54; wildlife destruction, 30

Catholic church: Catholic priest Almery, 50; church-sponsored unions for education programs, 32; church-state relations, 49; Conscientization term used by Catholic radicals, 36, 37, 48, 49, 53; cultural backwardness, 32; Cultural Extension Service, 32; Juventude Universitaria Catolica, 50; Movement for Basic Education (MEB), 32, 34, 39; progressives in the Church, 50; reconstruction of Brazilian society, 28; *Revolution through Peace,* 50-51; social institutions, 49; social reforms, 32, 95-96; socio-political change, 50; support to peasants and workers, 28, 32, 101; theologians, 50; universal principles, 50

Christianity: Adam's sin, 48; baptism, heresy and excommunication, 47; Biblical claims, as starting points of liberation theology, 48; book of Exodus, 49; bureaucratic organization, cadre of priests, hierarchy of authority, 53, 62; Catholicism, 53; children of God, hu-

141

mans as, 41–42; Christian commitment, 50; Christian historical ideal, 50; codified doctrines, 47, 53; denunciation of oppression by the prophets, 49; electronic and cybernetic age, 51; eternal reward or punishment, 42; evil in the world, 48; faith, 48; God as Creator and Father, 51; God's commandments, 48; God's kingdom, 48; God's (Father's) thrill of pride, 51; holiness, 52; human domination over nature, 88; human misery and Christian duty, 51; human selfishness, 51; Jesus Christ as saviour, 48; Jesus and non-attachment to material things and desire, 48; liberation theology, 28, 48, 49, 64–66, 105; life on earth preparatory and probationary period, 42; Old Testament, 49; original sin, 52; prophetic tradition, 49; radical Christianity, 54; salvation, 48, 50, 51, 65; second coming, 48; spiritual force of Christian continent, 51; syncretism, 53–54; wars of liberation, 66; worthiness, 41; Yahweh, 49

Comparison of concepts and theories, units: problem-type, 111; system-type, 111; topic-type, 111

Conscientization: abolition of class distinctions, 37, 38; anarchic economy, 37; "banking concept of education" ("digestive" or "nutritionist" approach), 36, 75; basic education movement, 99; belief in God, 64; change in socio-economic system, 38, 55, 65–66, 74, 81, 87–88; Communist party, organization, 66; critical approach to reality, 36–37, 74–75, 79; "dependency" theory, 65; dialectical understanding, 37; dignity of the oppressed, 36, 99; division of labour and wealth, 37, 55; *doxa* (opinion) to *logos* (knowledge), 36; economic, political, and cultural struggle, 64, 78; elimination of domination and exploitation, 37, 55–56, 65, 88, 92, 100 (*See also* Sarvodaya); encyclicals, *Mater et Magistra* and *pacem in Terris,* 50; engenhode acucar (sugar plantation), 29–30 (*See also* Catholic church); fatalism, 75; guerrilla warfare, 66; humanization of world, 74; magical explanations of oppression, 75; material security, 37; Marxist-Leninism, 66–67, 87; measures of alleviation, 74; ontological vocation, 36; oppression, morality, liberation and immortality in terms of cultural milieu, 49, 52, 55, 65–66, 78, 88, 94, 100; pacifist revolutionary, 51; paternalism, 36–37; power structures and relations, 37; *prise de conscience,* 36; process of knowledge, creation and transmission, 36, 75; proletarian condition, 37; protest movement, 6; psychological security, 37; radical theory of political education and action, 36; reform movement, 1–2; rehabilitation of labour, 37, 88; role of technology, 88, 100; self-development, 38, 99; socialization, 37, 95; social sin oppression, 65; solidarity, 37; state monopoly, 37, 96; transcendent dimension, 64; truth and the social dimension, 94

Conscientization, education: and illiterate landless labourers, 36, 37, 66, 74 (*See also* Brazil; Freire, Paulo); for consciousness raising, 9–10, 35–36, 66, 68–69, 74, 78–79, 98; for own culture by a cultural circle, 9–10

conceptual imperialism, 41

ethnocentrism, 105, 124

formal education as indoctrination, 72

Freire, Paulo: *abertura* (opening up), 35; adult literacy (Metado Paulo Freire), 34, 73, 74, 76; against traditional methods, of communication, 33; allies of workers, 75; Christian-Marxist dialogue, 53; class suicide, 75; critical reflection, 101; "cultural circles," 34, 74, 77, 78; cultural difference of East and West, 68, 100-101; cultural imperialism, 101; cultural invasion, 75, 100; culture of silence, 78, 79; dehumanizing bureaucrat, 52, 64, 88-89; demystification, 78; economic, political, and cultural realities, 76; educator-educatees, 75, 100; fanaticism, 79; generative themes, 77; historical struggle, 78, 101; humanistic orientation, 77; interest in theology, 51; Latin American theories of underdevelopment, 35; liberation education, 73, 78, 116; literacy campaign, 34; *Live through Struggle*, 76; Marxist, 32, 52; mutuality of the learning-teaching-learning process, 75; political democracy, 32, 66, 88 (*See also* Brazil, historical background); possibility of progress, 101; problematization, 77-78; radical catechism, 76; radio schools, 34; Recife cultural extension service, 34; revolutionary transformation of society, 52; right to rebellion, 52; scientific foundation of Freire's method, 77; syllabic language, codification of, 76-77; syllabic parts, 76; technocrats, 75; theology of revolution, 52; "third way" between capitalism and communism, 53, 83, 87-88; uniqueness of human being, 101; utopian vision, 78, 83

French Revolution, 117

Gandhian thought: abolition of state, 63, 88, 126; active versus passive learning, 71; acquisition of knowledge, 72; adult education, 72, 95-96; against abuse of caste system, 23, 83, 86, 88; Akhil Bharat Serv Seva Sangh (All-India Association to Serve All the People), 20; alienation, 70, 75, 85, 88, 89; animal and plant kingdom, 88; barter system, 94; basic education, 69-73, 75, 83; belief in *varna* system, 23 (*See also* Hinduism); change of social structure, 20-21, 61, 91, 93; closeness to nature, 88; communism without violence, 56; communism with God, 56; critique of foreign domination, 22 (*See also* India); *daridranarayana*, 22, 58, 88; decentralized structure, 20; decrease of material wants, 84, 88-89, 91; dialectical relationship, 91; equality of opportunity, 21; free labour, 86; Gandhian anarchism and ancient Indian political writings, 17-18, 21-23, 62, 96; God is truth, 43; "golden age," 57, 87; handicraft, 70, 84, 87, 94; harm of educational system (formal education), 69, 72, 95, 127-128; Hindustani Talimi Sangh, 21; home-spun yarn, 70, 72-73, 86 (*See also* Sarvodaya); India in villages, 22, 83, 86; Indian National Congress organization to be disbanded, 21; individual freedom, 84; institutional Gandhism, 20; inter-communal unity, 21; legislature, judiciary, executive, 84; Lok Seva Sangh (People's Servants Society), 21; lower creatures, 88; lower order, 88; material world and ideas, 91; metropolis-hinterland of Latin America, 22, 65; mother tongue versus foreign language in education, 70, 75; moral and religious ground for economic policy, 57, 85; *nai talim*, 21, 69, 73, 87, 93, 99; new India, 70; oceanic circle, 23, 85; *panchayati raj* (local self-government), 20, 84, 93; Peace Foundation in India and non-violence, 20; peasants, 86-87; pietistism and mysticism, 57; primary education, 69, 72; principle of correlation, 71; productive skill, 70, 84, 87, 94; psychological insight, 71, 99; purity of means, 46, 60; quality of life, 87; regressive form of education, 72; relationship of language to culture, 70; respect for manual labourers, 57, 93, 94 (*See also* Marxism); revolutionary Gandhism, 20, 23; ritual pollution, 23; ruralized school curriculum, 95; scientific attitude, 57, 72; self-contained villages, 21, 70, 83, 93-94; self-sufficiency, 86; sense of tranquility, 84; *Small is Beautiful,* 87; transmission of a society's values, 72, 91, 95, 127; treatment of untouchables, 61, 90; tyranny of English, 70; village republic, 22, 47, 53, 57, 63, 70, 83; (*See also* Sarvodaya); village guards, 84

Hinduism: *advaita,* 42, 56; *ahimsa, karmayoga,* and *dharma,* 44-45; *anaasakti* (non-attachment) and *aasakti* (attachment), 58-59, 69; *aparigraha* (the mental and social state of non-attachment to worldly possessions), 46; *atman,* brahman, and *avidya,* 45; *bhakti* (devotional), *nishkama karma,* and *karmayogi,* 44-45; Brahmanist, 42, 56; caste system, *jati* and *varna,* caste *dharma,* incarnation, 23, 42, 45, 47, 56-57, 86, 88, 96, 97, 105 (*See also* Gandhian thought); conceptual awareness of empirical world, 69; cycle of rebirth, 86, 88; *dharma,* 44-45; *duragraha, ahankara* (egotistic self-love), and *moksha* (salvation), 44, 47, 63-64 (*See also* Vinoba Bhave's thought); education that liberates, 69; empirical world, 69; *Gita* and *Upanishads,* 18; *grahasthashrama,* 59; higher knowledge, 69; *karmayogi,* 44-45; laws of *karma,* 42, 44, 57, 86; "love thine enemy," 44; *nishkamakarma,* 44; personal and local phenomenon, 62; pursuit of perfection, 45; proselytization, 62; principles of *Bhagavat Gita,* 43; radical Hinduism, 54; reformed Hinduism, 41; *sanyasi* (ascetic life), 44; *satyagraha* and *Sarvodaya,* 45, 46, 57; spiritual salvation, 42, 72; spiritual tradition of gift giving, 25; swastika, 57; *tapasya,* 43, 44; upward social mobility, 42

India: ancestral religion, 16; ethnic communities, languages, states, 4; exploitation of farmers, 25, 61, 88; foreign domination and resulting loss of "republican character," 22, 24, 75; indigenous cultures, 2, 3, 59, 75, 124; problem of Indian villages, 22

India, colonial rule: clerks and administrators, 69; colonial experience, 5, 63; colonization, 16, 97; exploitation of India, 22; imperial exploitation, 115 (*See also* industrialization); Indian National Congress, 15; Sepoy rebellion, 15; Thomas Babington Macaulay's Minute, 69

India, cultural and social change: colonial rule, 15; meritocratic basis of dynamic class stratification, 105; technology, 10, 67; social and public policy, 106

India, influence of communism: Communist party, 25, 61; Maoists, 61; Musahari Community Development Block, 61; Naxalites, 61; peasant movement, 61; People's Republic of China, 61; Soviet-style economic planning, 15; "Sovietized" villages, 25

India, influence of West: dependency theory, 6; Western capitalism, 6; Western education, 15, 24, 69; Western view of economic growth, 84

Industrialization, India and Brazil: back to nature, 89; benefits of technology, material comforts, 96, 116, 128-129; dehumanization, 89; development of culture, 82; economic and technological change, 128; formal education, 3, 69, 127-128; industrial civilization of West, 72; managing production and distribution, 81-82; metropolitan centers and cycles of poverty, 15, 22, 55; modern urban industrial society, 17, 55; new needs, 129; oppressive social institutions, 55, 59, 66-67; problems of massification and alienation, 22, 88-89; promoters of Conscientization, 89; respecting, eliminating, or modifying environmental constraints, 82; sapped creativity and responsibility, 72; science without wisdom, 82; secular and profane wisdom, 82; social harmony, 129; undemocratic management, 89; wisdom and science, 82

Marxism: anti-Christian materialism, 56; attributes of Indian thinking, 56; basic scientific laws, 57; bourgeoisie, 58, 63, 88, 89, 97; capitalist society, 58, 63, 89, 99; class, 58, 88, 93; classless society, 57, 58, 65; concentration of power, 63, 99; controlling institutions, 58, 62-63; dictatorship of the proletariat, 58, 64; economic growth, 59; individual as proprietor of own capacities, 59, 62; inevitability of human progress, 57, 58; injustice, 60, 63; intellectual freedom, 63; manual and mental labour, 58, 88, 94; Marxism, 10, 37, 52; Marxism and Sarvodaya, 56; moral suasion, 60; neo-Marxism, 60, 105; policy formation and implementation, 88; proliferation of wants, 59; property as theft, 62-64; realism, 60; respect for manual labourers compared to Marxist proletariate, 57-58, 70, 88; Sarvodaya minus God, 56; seizure of power, 59; scientific socialist, 58, 64; socialist dictatorship, 64; socio-economic arrangement, 60, 61; Soviet-style communism, 105

Marxism: structural violence, 60; surplus value, 58; violent confrontation, 60, 99; Western anarchism, 62-63

Mazeway, 8

nationalism, 10, 72

patronizing charity, 25

patron-client, 29

patron-dependent, 29, 34

political movements: capitalism, 124; communism, 124; Democracy, capitalist and state socialist system, 106; super power, 124

reductionism, 41

reform: cataclysmic, 117; collectivist mystique, 53; revolutionary upheavals, 1, 73-74, 126; revolutionary philosophy, 53

Religion: Buddhism, obedience and reverence, 15, 40; conduct and action, 40-41; humility, 125; image of perfection, 124; institutionalized religion, 124-125; Jaina scripture, 16; manifestation of faith, 40; omnipotence, 124; religious base and ethical principles, 40-41; religious inspiration, 124; syncretism, 53-54; theological and pastoral work, 47-48; transcendence of earthly existence, 125

Revitalization movement: challenges of Marxism and nationalism, 55; change in curriculum, 96; *China Pictorial,* 92; *China Reconstructs,* 92; construction of a satisfying culture, 6, 16, 40; corruptions and temptations of access to power, 125; cultural entities, 104; dominant economic and political elites, 95, 97, 124, 126, 128; equal opportunity and conditions to develop potential, 123 (*See also* Gandhian thought); Indian cultural revitalization movement, Sarvodaya and saryagraha, 18, 53, 83, 93; leaders and prophets, 4, 25, 41, 127; religious, political, and socio-cultural change, 92-93, 99, 109; Renaissance, 53; Sarvodaya and Conscientization as social movements, 55, 100; seven tasks to be accomplished, 7-8; stages: steady state, individual stress, cultural distortion, revitalization movements, 7; superiority of one race, ethnic group, social class, or gender, 123; techniques and cultural practices, 95

Sarvodaya: autonomous village republics, 47, 53, 57, 61, 63, 70, 83; class struggle, 66; classical liberal view, 59, 62-63; consensus formulation, 63; constitutional guarantees, 98; cooperation and harmony within castes or tribes, 96; decentralization of power, 47, 63; development of intellectual and spiritual potential, 27, 46-47, 55, 56, 68, 86; doctrine of trusteeship, 14, 21, 59, 60, 63, 97; egotism and altruism, 42-43, 46; evils of statism, 96; *Fors Clavigera* and bread labour, 17, 20, 86, 93, 94; freedom of speech, assembly, 98; Hindu and Buddhist ethical principles, 15; Human beings as inherently good, 96, 126; integration of East and West, 15-18; integral units, 85; *janshakhti* (people's power), 63; labour, 88, 89; leveling of rich and poor, 13-14, 55, 57, 86, 96; liberal democratic stance, 98; *lokniti* (people's justice), 63; material improvement, 91, 93; middle class, 98, 100; moral superiority, 65-66; multiclass movement, 97; nativistic movement (*Swadeshi*), 16, 63 (*See also* Gandhian thought); need of Sarvodaya as a revolutionary non-state society, 96, 126; physical elimination of political enemies, 98; protest movements: Bhoodan, Gramdan, sampatidan and shramdan, 6, 9, 25-26, 92; pursuit of power, 59; Quakers (Society of Friends), 63; reform movement, 1, 56; representative democracy, 85; revolutionary change, 21-22; sacrifice of privacy, 97; *samadhi* (state of ecstacy), 42; *satya* and *ahimsa*, 13, 45 (*See also satyagraha*); selfless service, 91, 94; semi-feudal bondage, 62, 93; sense of self-worth, 91; small-scale socio-political units, 64, 96-97; social action, 13, 20; social divisions, 58; social ethics, 62, 65-66; social relations, 62; socialistic pattern of society, 97; spiritual potential, 27, 46, 47, 55, 56, 68, 86; struggle for mutual service, 20, 57, 63; technology to improve people's lives, 88, 94; traditional India, 17, 47; uneven land distribution, 62; unlawful arrest, 98; vested interests, 85; villages as locus of governments, 85; Weberian notions of social class, 58; welfare of all, 18, 46-47, 55

satyagraha: holding fast to the truth, process of praxis, 18, 60, 78; mutuality of respect, 98; non-violence, non-cooperation, and civil disobedience, 21, 59, 60, 64, 83-84, 98, 126; *satya* and *ahimsa*, 13, 45 (*See also* Sarvodaya); self-awareness, self-purification, and individual *dharma*, 12-13, 43, 97 (*See also* Hinduism)

Scientists: behavioural scientist, 107; scientific knowledge, 107; social scientist, 106, 107

temperocentrism, 105-106, 124

Third World, 2, 6, 52; oppression in former colonies (neo-colonies), 75, 108

Values: value free, 106; value neutral, 106; social values, 106-107; scientific values, 106-107

Vinoba Bhave's thought: abolition of caste-system, 23; against colonial rule, 24; Bhoodan pilgrimage, 73; enlightened anarchy, 23, 62; Hindu *weltanchauung,* 47; individualism, 63 (*See also* Hinduism); *karmayogi,* 114; *padyatra* to pursue landlords, 25-26; partyless democracy, 63, 96; promoter of Bhoodan, *Shramdan, Budhidan,* 26-27 (*See also* Sarvodaya); religion as truth, 42; results of slavery, 24 (*See also* India); saint-politician, 114; *samya-yoga* as revolutionary philosophy, 43, 114; selfless service, 63; spiritual potential, 27, 42; troubled with calm of stagnation, 23; trusteeship in terms of village or local community, 23

Violence or non-violence as process of conversion, 14, 38, 39, 61, 99, 116; psychological violence, 99

West: pre-industrial Europe, 89

ABOUT THE AUTHOR

Mathew Zachariah was born in the princely state of Travancore (now part of Kerala) in India. He teaches comparative education and sociology of education in the Department of Educational Policy and Administrative Studies (Faculty of Education) at the University of Calgary in Canada. He received his bachelor's degree in economics and his Bachelor of Education degree from the Universities of Madras and Delhi, respectively. He has a master's degree from State University College, New Paltz, New York, and a Ph.D. degree from the University of Colorado, Boulder. His publications have appeared in several books and scholarly publications.

Zachariah's service responsibilities have included headship of the Department of Educational Foundations at the University of Calgary. In 1978-79, he was president of the Comparative and International Education Society (USA). Currently, he is on the board of directors of the Shastri Indo-Canadian Institute and on the advisory editorial board of *Comparative Education Review*.